INNOVATIVE FEDERAL CONTRACTING

CASE STUDIES

GOVERNMENT PROCEDURES AND OPERATIONS

Additional books in this series can be found on Nova's website under the Series tab.

Additional e-books in this series can be found on Nova's website under the e-book tab.

GOVERNMENT PROCEDURES AND OPERATIONS

INNOVATIVE FEDERAL CONTRACTING

CASE STUDIES

DARREL COBB
EDITOR

publishers

New York

Additional color graphics may be available in the e-book version of this book.

Library of Congress Cataloging-in-Publication Data

ISBN: 978-1-63463-440-3

Published by Nova Science Publishers, Inc. † *New York*

CONTENTS

PREFACE

This book discusses the innovative contracting case studies, and provides a legal overview of the competition in federal contracting.

Chapter 1 - *Innovative Contracting Case Studies* is an iterative, evolving document that describes a number of ways Federal agencies are getting more innovation per taxpayer dollar – all under existing laws and regulations.

The White House Office of Science and Technology Policy (OSTP) and the Office of Management and Budget's Office of Federal Procurement Policy (OFPP) seek to encourage greater innovation in Federal contracting. In this spirit, OSTP has compiled this collection of agency case studies to highlight different models that have been successfully tested by agencies to meet a range of needs related to research, prototyping, and market testing.

Chapter 2 - Competition in federal procurement contracting has long been of interest to Congress and the executive branch, in part because of the belief that increased competition among potential vendors results in lower prices for the government. President Obama issued a memorandum calling for increased competition in federal contracting on March 4, 2009, shortly after taking office, and his Administration has sought to reduce the number of "noncompetitive" contracts by various means, including by issuing guidance on "Increasing Competition and Structuring Contracts for Best Results" in October 2009. Most recently, the Department of Defense (DOD), which generally accounts for nearly 70% of federal procurement spending per year, began implementing regulations that would promote competition by generally requiring contracting officers to re-solicit agency requirements if a solicitation allowed fewer than 30 days for the receipt of proposals and resulted in only one bid or offer.

The Competition in Contracting Act (CICA) of 1984 generally governs competition in federal procurement contracting. Any procurement contract not entered into through the use of procurement procedures expressly authorized by a particular statute is subject to CICA. CICA requires that contracts be entered into after "full and open competition through the use of competitive procedures" unless certain circumstances exist that would permit agencies to use noncompetitive procedures. Full and open competition can be obtained through the use of sealed bids, competitive proposals, or other procures defined as competitive under CICA (e.g., procurement of architectural or engineering services under the Brooks Act). Full and open competition under CICA also encompasses "full and open competition after exclusion of sources," such as results when agencies engage in dual sourcing or set aside acquisitions for small businesses.

Any contract entered into without full and open competition is noncompetitive, but noncompetitive contracts can still be in compliance with CICA when circumstances permitting other than full and open competition exist. CICA recognizes seven such circumstances, including (1) single source for goods or services; (2) unusual and compelling urgency; (3) maintenance of the industrial base; (4) requirements of international agreements; (5) statutory authorization or acquisition of brand-name items for resale; (6) national security; and (7) contracts necessary in the public interest. CICA also allows agencies to use "special simplified procedures" when acquiring goods or services whose expected value is less than $150,000, or commercial goods or services whose expected value is less than $6.5 million ($12 million in emergencies).

Issuance of orders under task order and delivery order (TO/DO) contracts is not subject to CICA, although award of TO/DO contracts is. However, the Federal Acquisition Streamlining Act (FASA) of 1994 established a preference for multiple-award TO/DO contracts; required that agencies provide contractors "a fair opportunity" to compete for orders in excess of $3,000 under multiple-award contracts; and authorized the Government Accountability Office (GAO) to hear protests challenging the issuance of task or delivery orders that increase the scope, period, or maximum value of the underlying contract. The National Defense Authorization Act (NDAA) for FY2008 further limited the use of single-award TO/DO contracts. It also specified what constitutes a "fair opportunity to be considered" for orders in excess of $5.5 million under multiple-award contracts and granted GAO exclusive jurisdiction to hear protests of orders valued in excess of $10 million that do not increase the scope, period, or maximum value of the contract.

This jurisdiction is permanent as to protests of defense agency contracts (P.L. 112-239), but only lasts through September 30, 2016, for protests of civilian agency contracts (P.L. 112-81).

In: Innovative Federal Contracting: Case Studies   ISBN: 978-1-63463-440-3
Editor: Darrel Cobb   © 2015 Nova Science Publishers, Inc.

Chapter 1

INNOVATIVE CONTRACTING CASE STUDIES[*]

Office of Science Technology Policy and the Office of Management and Budget

INTRODUCTION

Innovative Contracting Case Studies is an iterative, evolving document that describes a number of ways Federal agencies are getting more innovation per taxpayer dollar – all under existing laws and regulations.

The White House Office of Science and Technology Policy (OSTP) and the Office of Management and Budget's Office of Federal Procurement Policy (OFPP) seek to encourage greater innovation in Federal contracting. In this spirit, OSTP has compiled this collection of agency case studies to highlight different models that have been successfully tested by agencies to meet a range of needs related to research, prototyping, and market testing.

Note that OSTP compiled these case studies based in part on feedback from external experts, and that this *Innovative Contracting Case Studies* document does not necessarily reflect the views of the Federal departments and agencies cited as examples. The availability and use of different innovative contracting methods will require consideration of available legal authorities and the desired outcome/goals of the specific activity.

---

[*] This is an edited, reformatted and augmented version of a document issued August 2014.

These agency case studies are intended as a resource, not a directive or policy, to facilitate creative problem solving in the public interest.

Background

Over the years, much progress has been made to help Federal agencies gain greater access to the innovation and synergies generated by the commercial marketplace. Despite this progress, the standard procurement processes that agencies rely on to meet most of their needs may remain highly complex and enigmatic for companies that are not traditional government contractors. Many of these companies can offer Federal agencies valuable new ways of solving long-standing problems and cost- effective alternatives for meeting everyday needs. As budgetary constraints continue to reduce available resources, there is a heightened need to grow new innovative contracting models that can help agencies reach these entrepreneurs, and can reduce the complexity and cost of doing business with the government. Such tools allow Federal agencies to pay contractors for results, not just best efforts.

Current authorities in the Federal Acquisition Regulation (FAR) provide a variety of pathways that allow agencies to reshape existing processes to reduce transaction costs while still operating within the confines of existing law and regulation. Other new authorities, such as the America COMPETES Act, provide additional alternatives. In recent years, a number of agencies have conducted pilots to see how these authorities can help them acquire technology needs more efficiently and effectively.

In addition, this document includes a summary of three general approaches to innovative contracting that complement the five specific tools above:

- **Other Transactions:** A method of providing the flexibility needed to engage commercial companies that are not traditional government contractors.
- **FIRE/FIST:** An overall approach to procurement and program management that values speed, thrift, simplicity, and self-control.
- **Agile:** Short, frequent, iterative development cycles, with working software delivered at the end of each cycle.

Main Focus	Description
Discovering novel solutions	The *"incentive prize"* tool uses new authorities provided by the America COMPETES Reauthorization Act of 2010 to enable an agency to run a competition where the winner receives a prize for developing a viable solution to solve a government need. Since this model uses authority outside of the Federal Acquisition Regulation to test the market, it can help an agency reach beyond traditional contractors and increase the number of entities working to tackle a problem. The *"milestone-based competition"* process allows agencies to enter into contractual relationships with a qualified pool of contractors and to issue task orders for a series of clear, technically feasible milestones, each with an assigned deadline and monetary value.
Proving innovative solutions	The *"rapid technology prototyping"* model involves issuance of several contracts for small, inexpensive prototypes to be built within a short period of time (i.e., several months) and then tested in a relevant demonstration scenario to assess the viability of each prior to making a substantial investment. The *"challenge-based acquisition"* model is designed to explore the market and pay only for a successful solution, but is geared towards projects where solutions are likely to already exist as opposed to having to be developed. The key differentiator between challenge-based acquisition and a traditional performance- based acquisition is the firm requirement to demonstrate product performance in real-world conditions prior to a major commitment of resources for full production.
Scaling proven solutions	The *"staged contract"* method utilizes short concept papers to enable agencies to identify vendors who are most likely to receive an award and to help those who are less likely to receive an award avoid the cost of developing a detailed proposal.

Resources for Feedback and Collaboration

Innovative Contracting Case Studies is intended to be an iterative, evolving document, where frequent changes are welcome and expected. We encourage both private sector contractors and public servants to engage in a sustained discussion to identify new case studies and to improve this document's usefulness in future iterations.

OSTP and OFPP invite agencies to use the following resources to provide feedback, share experiences, and offer additional strategies that might be used to foster greater and more affordable innovation in the federal marketplace:

- Public discussion forum on innovative Federal government procurement practices
- Feds-only " Buyers Club" email group (open to all.gov and .mil email addresses)
- The TechFAR Handbook and Digital Services Playbook, focused on information technology acquisition

Acknowledgements

OSTP also would like to thank the many experts who helped develop these case studies, including:

Scott Anderson, MITRE Corporation (formerly)
Michael Arendt, MITRE Corporation
Courtney H. Bailey, NASA
Jonah Czerwinski, Department of Veterans Affairs (formerly)
Rick Dunn, DARPA (formerly)
Martin Edwards, MITRE Corporation
Gregory Godbout, General Services Administration
Mary Ann Lapham, Carnegie Mellon University
Patrick Littlefield, Department of Veterans Affairs
Carol Lundquist, National Security Agency
Carol Newcomb, Department of Veterans Affairs
Ryan Novak, MITRE Corporation
Jennifer Pahlka, OSTP (formerly)
Dan Ward, U.S. Air Force
Richard Weatherly, MITRE Corporation

George Xenofos, NASA
Andrew Yang, OSTP (formerly)

SUMMARIES

Rapid Technology Prototyping Contracts

What are Rapid Technology Prototyping Contracts?

A rapid technology prototyping contract is an innovative contracting model that consists of multiple, small, fast, and cheap acquisitions to "try out" innovative technologies. This is done by having companies develop prototypes applying the new technology to relevant demonstration scenarios within a defined timeframe. Rapid technology prototyping contracts may be used by the government for the rapid and inexpensive assessment of many cutting-edge, unproven, but potentially transformative technologies. Because substantial gains in innovation are often accompanied by substantial trial and error on big ideas, a realistic expectation for success rates in terms of establishing follow-on projects is only 10% to 30%.

What are the implications of Rapid Technology Prototyping Contracts?

- **For program managers:** Rapid technology prototyping contracts provide program managers with the ability to rapidly assess potentially transformative technologies without substantial government investment. The initial three to six month prototype projects can be done as Firm Fixed Price contracts that are executed in the company's own facilities. This eliminates cost risk to the government and emphasizes that the project is a test to see if the company can deliver a working prototype on schedule and budget. Using the company's own facility eliminates extra costs or delays associated with using a government facility for the development work. Rapid and cheap prototype assessment ensures decisions regarding additional investment of government resources are results-driven and significantly reduce the cost, schedule and technology risks for any subsequent work.

- **For legal:** Rapid technology prototyping contracts focus on rapid prototyping within existing frameworks, thereby creating new opportunities for efficiency using long-standing, well-tested laws and Federal Acquisition Regulations (e.g., FAR Parts 35 and 15).
- **For offerors:** Rapid technology prototyping contracts provide innovators, small businesses, and academia with accessible opportunities to pursue cutting-edge prototyping with minimal risk, expectations, and liability. Selected offerors are in regular communication with technical end users in the government, and therefore gain a better understanding of government needs that can be beneficial in future contracts, regardless of the prototype's outcome. Furthermore, should a prototype succeed, offerors can be selected for follow-on work through standard acquisition processes or another innovative contracting model.

What are the benefits of Rapid Technology Prototyping Contracts?

Rapid technology prototyping contracts can be very effective for quickly and cheaply assessing many potential new technologies to identify viable options to meet an agency's particular requirements. This approach, which uses the Broad Agency Announcement (BAA) acquisition method, can easily be tailored and customized to meet the specific requirements and constraints of different government agencies. Among the innovative contracting models, Rapid Technology Prototyping contracts can uniquely:

- Encourage small businesses to partner with academia to transform basic research developments into applied research that could potentially be used to address the government's requirements.
- Facilitate knowledge transfer from the government to small businesses to better enable the small business to support the government's requirements.
- Effectively utilize limited government resources to rapidly assess many technologies and make results-based decisions regarding further investment.

What are the results or case studies to date?

Rapid technology prototyping has been used by the Department of Defense with respect to 3D mapping prototypes of urban terrain, for radio detection finder systems, and for sensor mechanisms that detect improvised explosive devices and provide warnings to ground forces.

STAGED CONTRACTS

What are Staged Contracts?

A staged contract is an innovative contracting model that follows a three-phase evaluation process consisting of a short concept paper, invite-only full proposal, and subsequent 1-2 year pilot evaluation. Staged contracts may be used by the government for the rapid and inexpensive assessment of many existing or prototype private-sector technologies. Staged contracts, by forgoing the extensive requirements of traditional acquisition processes in favor of short concept papers, let agencies sample the diverse technology landscape for potential solutions. These concept papers allow Broad Agency Announcement (BAA) respondents to communicate the essence of their proposal without expending undue time and effort. In this way, staged contracts reduce administrative burden for both offerors and agencies. In general, staged contracts work as follows:

1. *Announce:* agencies release a broad solicitation for contractors to submit short concept papers communicating the essence of their proposed technologies.
2. *Study:* agencies invite promising offerors to submit detailed full proposals with both technical and cost/price components.
3. *Evaluate:* agencies evaluate selected full proposals in 1-2 year pilots, during which there is ample opportunity for offerors to communicate with end users and refine their technology.
4. *Deploy:* agencies decide to deploy, terminate, or further evaluate pilots.

What Are the Implications of Staged Contracts?

- **For program managers:** Staged contracts rapidly funnel the landscape of promising private sector technologies into rigorously evaluated pilots to inform potential agency-wide deployment. Quickly filtering the submissions lets program managers identify the most promising technologies with strong potential for wide impact, and invite these applicants to submit a full proposal for subsequent pilot testing. The evaluation of the technology allows decisions regarding additional investment of government resources to be results-driven and can significantly reduce the cost, time, and technology risks for subsequent scale-up work.

- **For legal:** The authority to solicit BAAs for staged contracts is outlined under the provisions of Parts 35.016 and 6.102(d)(2)(i) of the Federal Acquisition Regulation (FAR), which provides for the competitive selection of proposals submitted in response to the BAA. Accordingly, proposals selected for award must be considered the result of full and open competition and fully compliant with Public Law 98-369 (The Competition in Contracting Act of 1984). Staged contract BAAs are furthermore only an expression of interest and thus do not commit the government to make an award or pay proposal preparation costs.
- **For offerors:** Staged contracts provide offerors an accessible way to do business with government. Staged contracts require offerors to submit only an initial summary slide and eight- page concept paper instead of the hundreds of pages expected in traditional acquisition processes. This accessible, staged evaluation process helps ensure that successful offerors' core competencies lie not in proposal drafting but in delivering technology solutions.

Moreover, the brief and open-ended BAA of staged contracts encourages small business participation with its simplicity and emphasis on contractor creativity.

What Are the Benefits of Staged Contracts?

Staged contracts can be very effective at rapidly funneling many private sector technologies to both effectively identify and validate options for meeting an agency's particular requirements. This approach, which uses the BAA acquisition method, can be easily tailored and customized to meet the specific requirements and constraints of different government agencies. Among the innovative contracting models, staged contracts can uniquely:

- Harness the ingenuity of the American people to provide government solutions through less burdensome concept papers.
- Effectively utilize limited government resources to rapidly assess many technologies and make results-based decisions regarding further investment.

- Facilitate knowledge transfer from the government to small businesses, especially during pilots, to better enable the small businesses to support the government's requirements.
- Ensure extensive agency end user involvement, buy-in, and subsequent technology adoption.

What Are the Results or Case Studies to Date?

The Department of Veterans Affairs Innovation Initiative (VAi2) Industry Innovation Competition illustrates the promise of staged contracts. The VAi2 Competition staged contracts followed a three- phase process consisting of an eight-page concept paper, 50-page invite-only full proposal, and 1-2 year pilot evaluation. The VAi2 BAA—spanning only 22 pages, including appendices and references—was issued under the FAR. The 2012 VAi2 BAA hosted topic areas ranging from "Women's Health: Maternity Tracker" to "Prevention and Treatment of Pressure Ulcers" to "Mobile Technology and Applications for Veteran Benefits." The VAi2 competition has awarded no fewer than 135 solutions worth $102.5 million, fielded solutions in eight topic areas, received over 20,000 ideas from 600 industry offerors, and collaborated with over 100 subject matter experts. Below are specific pilot projects funded through the VAi2 Competition:

1. **VETransfer:** With a BAA award, the VA Center for Innovation (VACI) provided seed funding to VETransfer, a non-profit startup, to create an end-to-end business accelerator for Veteran entrepreneurs, offering individualized mentorship at a physical incubator facility as well as online resources. In its first years since 2011, VETransfer generated 24 startups, raised nearly $1.4 million, created 89 jobs, and is scaling nationwide. Moreover, around 400 Veterans have completed the three-month online programs.

2. **Agilex Technologies:** Agilex Technologies developed a system that enables providers to access electronic health record information on mobile devices. Most pilot participants reported a positive impact on their productivity and ability to communicate with patients and other providers. The pilot also demonstrated the feasibility of deploying mobile devices in a clinical setting on VA networks.

3. **MedRed's TBI Toolbox:** MedRed's TBI Toolbox enables care providers to continuously develop, share, and administer the latest

treatment methods in the rapidly evolving field of polytrauma care. Pilot users project the TBI Toolbox will eliminate collection of over 19,000 paper forms per year if deployed across the VA enterprise.

MILESTONE-BASED COMPETITIONS

What are Milestone-Based Competitions?

A milestone-based competition is an innovative contracting model that promotes competition among a stable pool of selected offerors across a series of clear, technically feasible milestones, with payment withheld until the associated, agreed-upon milestone is completed. In crafting the solicitation, the government establishes a series of milestones, each with well-defined requirements, a deadline, and an assigned monetary value. Milestone-based competitions should be used by the Government to attract businesses with innovative approaches to well-defined, multi-component problems. In general, competitive milestone-based contracts work as follows:

1. *Announce:* agencies release a broad solicitation for contractors to compete through a series of milestones, each with a defined problem statement and monetary value.
2. *Select:* agencies select a pool of competing contractors following the initial solicitation.
3. *Launch:* agencies announce which milestones are under competition and provide more specific language on technical constraints and deadlines.
4. *Maintain:* agencies award first milestone winners and decide when to place the remaining milestones under competition, depending on fiscal constraints. The government is not compelled to compete any milestones beyond the first, and no contractor is entitled to award money beyond the minimum.

What Are the Implications of Milestone-Based Competitions?

- **For program managers:** Milestone-based competitions provide program managers the ability to attract innovative approaches to well-documented problems, while minimizing cost, risk, and liability.

Competitive milestone-based contracts, by forgoing a bulky, long-term deliverable in favor of a series of achievable milestones, encourage participation from small businesses and high-growth startups. The unique combination of attributes in these contracts—firm-fixed price, indefinite delivery/indefinite quantity (IDIQ), and performance incentives—maximizes value delivered to government and places full financial responsibility on the contractors.

- **For legal:** The authority to solicit Broad Agency Announcements (BAA) for milestone-based competitions is allowed by Federal Acquisition Regulation (FAR) Part 35. Milestone-based competition BAAs are furthermore only an expression of interest and thus do not commit the government to make an award or pay proposal preparation costs. The NASA ILDD program (detailed below) drew further authority from NASA FAR Supplement (NFS) Part 1835.

- **For offerors:** The simplicity, transparency, and clear, technically feasible series of requirements surrounding competitive milestone-based competitions encourage participation from traditionally underrepresented contractors, such as small businesses and high-growth startups. Selected offerors can also leverage the credibility of government to attract additional private investment tied to government-established milestones. This synergy would amplify incentives to deliver maximum value to government, financially strengthen competitors, and catalyze industry innovation.

What Are the Benefits of Milestone-Based Competitions?

Milestone-based competitions are very effective at attracting innovative solutions from small businesses to address well-documented problems, while minimizing government cost, risk, and liability. Milestone- based competitions also offer resource-constrained government agencies significant flexibility in funding and solicitation. For funding, agencies may choose which milestones to put in play and withhold others depending on financial circumstances. As each milestone is independent of another, agencies have no ongoing liabilities following the conclusion of one milestone, and possess the flexibility to modify or freeze the contract. For solicitation, the initial BAA need only contain the statement of objectives, baseline requirements, and property/data rights; the details of individual milestones can be augmented with greater specificity later, once the contractor pool is established. The same applies to future milestones not currently underway.

Competitive milestone-based contracts may also be more cost-effective than traditional contracts. For example, the NASA ILDD contracts (detailed below), under their first milestone "Critical Component Demonstration," paid only $500,000 rather than the typical $3-5 million for propulsion data from innovative rocket injectors using green propellants. Among the innovative contracting models, competitive milestone-based competitions can uniquely:

- Strengthen small businesses through more accessible financing and recruitment of private investment.
- Maximize value and innovation delivered to government on specific, concrete agency challenges.
- Ensure government flexibility in financing and solicitation given limited resources.

What Are the Results or Case Studies to Date?

The NASA Innovative Lunar Demonstrations Data (ILDD) program illustrates the promise of competitive milestone-based contracts. The NASA ILDD program intends to purchase specific data related to lunar exploration resulting from commercial development of small, robotic lunar landers. The NASA ILDD program awards small, firm-fixed price, indefinite delivery/indefinite quantity (IDIQ) contracts over the course of five years, with a total value of as much as $30.1 million. Multiple awards are possible, with a minimum data purchase of $10,000 for each selected contractor. Individual awardees can earn as much as $10.1 million.

With an open-ended 18-page BAA, the program attracted underrepresented organizations, including small businesses, non-profits, new startups, and university consortia, before ultimately selecting six teams. All six teams are participating in the Google Lunar X PRIZE, which provides a total of $30 million in prizes to privately funded teams to safely land a robot on the moon's surface, have the robot traverse 500 meters, and send data back to Earth. Moreover, the six teams participating in the NASA ILDD program were not established contractors; though most had identified private investors and crafted a business case, none had ever contracted with the government. The NASA ILDD program also encouraged significant private investment tied to government-established milestones: several competitors had private investments dependent on the successful completion of NASA milestones.

INCENTIVE PRIZES

What Are Incentive Prizes?

An incentive prize is a contracting model that promotes innovation by offering a reward upon completion of a specific objective task. Prizes enable the Federal government to pay only for success, establish an ambitious goal, and reach beyond the "usual suspects" to increase the number of minds tackling a problem without having to predict which team or approach is most likely to succeed. Many well-known incentive prizes have focused on catalyzing technology R&D, though prize administrators are increasingly using incentive prizes to drive behavior change, market adoption of existing solutions and interventions, and progress in areas of social policy such as health, energy use, and education.

What Are The Implications of Incentive Prizes?

- **For program managers:** Incentive prizes offer resource-constrained program managers a cost-effective tool to spur innovative solutions to clearly-defined challenges. In addition to only paying the winner, well-structured prizes can drive cumulative competitor investment totaling 10-40 times the prize purse. Program managers can use prizes to: attract new ideas; build prototypes and launch pilots; stimulate markets; raise awareness; mobilize action; and inspire transformation.[1] Program managers can choose from a variety of different prize types to achieve different types of goals, including: exemplar, point-solution, market stimulation, exposition, participation, and network prizes.[2]
- **For legal:** Section 24 of the Stevenson-Wydler Technology Innovation Act of 1980, 15 U.S.C. §3719, as enacted by the America COMPETES Reauthorization Act of 2010, permits any agency head to "carry out a program to award prizes competitively to stimulate innovation that has the potential to advance the mission of the respective agency" (§24(b)). Section 24 authorizes agencies to use

both private sector and Federal appropriated funds in order to design prizes, administer prizes, and offer monetary awards for prize competitions.

- **For offerors:** Incentive prizes reduce bureaucratic obstacles to innovation by attracting and focusing competitors of all backgrounds to address a well-defined challenge in pursuit of a prize and acclaim. Incentive prizes offer innovators a clear target to shoot for, generate substantial public and industry support, and require far less paperwork than traditional acquisition processes. Beyond the award, incentive prizes can also create value for contestants by encouraging the development of new skills as well as problem-solving networks that may have beneficial effects beyond the competition.

What Are the Benefits of Incentive Prizes?

Prize administrators in the public sector are reaping the rewards of well-designed incentive prizes. Specifically, prizes enable the Federal government to:

- **Pay only for success and establish an ambitious goal without having to predict which team or approach is most likely to succeed.** Contracts and grants are awarded based on proposals for future work, forcing agencies to value past performance at the expense of disruptive innovation. With a focus on proven results, prizes empower untapped talent to deliver unexpected solutions to tough problems.
- **Reach beyond the "usual suspects" to increase the number of minds tackling a problem.** Prizes can tap the top talent and best ideas wherever they lie, sourcing breakthroughs from a broad pool of innovation in a given industry.
- **Bring out-of-discipline perspectives to bear.** Empirical research conducted by Harvard Business School[3] finds that breakthrough solutions are most likely to come from outside the scientific discipline or at the intersection of two fields of study.
- **Increase cost-effectiveness to maximize the return on taxpayer dollars.** As teams compete not just for the cash purse, but also for the associated validation, prestige, and satisfaction that results from

solving important problems, prizes incent significant additional investment, leveraging the prize purse's impact.

- **Inspire risk-taking by offering a level playing field through credible rules and robust judging mechanisms.** Prizes give entrepreneurs and innovators license to pursue an endorsed stretch goal that otherwise would have been considered overly audacious. Clear target metrics and validation protocols defined for the judging of a prize can themselves become defining tools for the subject industry or field.

What Are the Results or Case Studies to Date?

- **Astronaut Glove Challenge**. Before entrepreneur Peter Homer and his startup spacesuit company Flagsuit LLC won NASA's $450,000 prize purse in 2009 for designing a flexible glove better than those in use by NASA's astronauts, he had been a satellite designer, sailmaker, microgravity experiment designer, and local community center director. Since winning the competition, Flagsuit LLC has continued to grow, obtaining contracts with Orbital Outfitters in 2007 to supply gloves for their Industrial Suborbital Spacesuit being manufactured for XCOR and signing a sole source, prime contract in 2011 with NASA to develop and test improved spacesuit glove assemblies.
- **Wendy Schmidt Oil Cleanup X Challenge.** The $1.4 million 2011 competition, supported by technical expertise from the Department of Interior and the National Oceanic and Atmospheric Administration (NOAA), inspired entrepreneurs, engineers, and scientists worldwide to develop innovative, rapidly deployable, and highly efficient methods of cleaning up oil spills from the ocean surface. The winner, Elastec/American Marine – a growing Illinois-based manufacturer of oil spill and environmental equipment that uses local talent for nearly all its fabrication – recovered oil at a rate more than three times the best previously recorded in controlled conditions.
- **Vehicle Stopper Challenge**. This 2011 Air Force Research Laboratory (AFRL) competition focused on a problem that had vexed military security forces and civilian police for years: how to safely stop uncooperative fleeing vehicles without causing permanent damage to the vehicle or harming any of the occupants. Through this competition, AFRL was able to multiply the number of people

thinking about this problem over 100-fold and received a workable solution within a 60-day period. For a $25,000 purse, a retired 66-year-old mechanical engineer from Lima, Peru submitted the winning solution.

CHALLENGE BASED ACQUISITIONS

What Are Challenge-Based Acquisitions?

Challenge-Based Acquisitions provide for the introduction of innovative and cost-saving technologies into existing acquisition programs through "challenge" proposals. With a challenge-based acquisition, an agency can incentivize private-sector entities to develop and demonstrate their solutions in real-world conditions as a source selection mechanism for the award of contracts or task orders for additional testing, refinement, or production of their proposed solution. The award of contracts and task orders occurs if, and only if, the private-sector entity successfully meets the real-world requirements of the challenge.

With a Challenge-Based Acquisitions, the agency must:

- *Determine the user's need and decompose complex requirements.* The government must first determine the user's need, and then interpret this need into a series of requirements which can be translated into meaningful challenge events. This provides industry with the maximum opportunity to develop and propose an innovative solution.
- *Communicate user experience and needs to industry.* The government must explain the scope of the challenge to industry by describing how it will evaluate challenge event participation in the same or similar environment for which the solution will ultimately be used.
- *Design and execute the challenge event.* The government must design the challenge event, including the plan on how the challenge event will be executed contractually, specific requirements for challenge participation, and detailed evaluation criteria for successful performance and award of follow-on contracts or task orders.
- *Analyze the challenge results and provide contract or task order awards.* The government must use quantitative and qualitative measurements to evaluate challenge results during or immediately

after the challenge, and/or over a longer term, as defined by the initial challenge description contained in the Request for Proposal (RFP). These results are then used to determine follow-on contract or task-order awards.

Applicability

It is important to determine whether a challenge-based acquisition approach is appropriate to address Government needs. The acquisition team should evaluate the current state of its program against the characteristics listed below:

- Has rapid schedule demands or is responding to an urgent requirement,
- Responds to incremental capability needs,
- Is small from an Acquisition Category (ACAT) perspective or is not a program of record,
- Is a sub-system or component of a larger system or acquisition,
- Depends on emerging or uncertain technology,
- Seeks attention of non-traditional innovation sources,
- Expects a short product life cycle or rapid refresh rate,
- Has a clear acquisition quantity and price,
- Requires simultaneous industry and Government solution discovery, or
- Wishes to pay only for results.

What Are the Implications of Challenge-Based Acquisitions?

- **For program managers:** Challenge-Based Acquisitions allow for the evaluation of a solution in a similar environment to the user, thus permitting major investment decisions of government resources to be results-driven. This can significantly reduce the cost, schedule, and performance risks for the technology being acquired.
- **For legal advisors:** Challenge-Based Acquisitions use the authority of FAR Parts 15 and 35, which provide for the competitive selection of proposals submitted in response to a competitive solicitation or BAA. Accordingly, selection of proposals for award via a Challenge-

Based Acquisition approach must be considered to be the result of full and open competition.

- **For offerors**: With Challenge-Based Acquisitions, the government is not defining a specified solution for a given capability need, but is asking industry to propose what it believes to be the best solution to address the capability need. This means that small businesses and other new or non-traditional offerors may submit solutions for evaluation based on their actual performance at a challenge event thus leveling the playing field for those vendors not familiar with the government contracting environment.

What Are the Benefits of Challenge-Based Acquisition?

Using challenges as a source selection mechanism and part of a larger acquisition framework allows maximum flexibility for industry to innovate. Challenge-based acquisition does not ask industry to respond to a prescriptive specification or presupposed solution. Instead, industry is free to propose any solution they believe will meet the challenge criteria. The government will then use the challenge event to assess proven performance before a major commitment of resources is made (e.g. production level buy). As a result, challenge-based acquisition helps ensure that the government buys the right thing, buys it the right way, and does this the first time by minimizing investment of major resources upfront before a solution has proven itself.

What Are the Results or Case Studies to Date?

Culvert Denial Challenge

In August 2014, the Joint Improvised Explosive Device Defeat Organization (JIEDDO) awarded a multiple award IDIQ contract for the JIEDDO Culvert Denial Challenge. Through this IDIQ, the government seeks innovative technical solutions for surveillance and inspection of Improvised Explosive Device (IED) emplacements in and around culverts. Ten vendors will participate in a Surveillance Challenge event and another 10 vendors will participate in an Inspection Challenge event. The 20 vendors will compete on a Ft. Benning, GA training range in October 2014.

2012 Counter-IED Robotics Challenge

The JIEDDO Counter-IED Robotics Challenge was held in June, 2012, at Fort Benning, GA. The challenge had four independent events: Endurance, Reconnaissance, Detect, and Disrupt. The Endurance Challenge assessed the speed and endurance of mounted, dismounted, and portable unmanned ground vehicles over an improved road. Reconnaissance assessed sensor acuity, platform mobility and spatial accuracy of small robots required to locate objects in a tactical environment. The Detect Challenge assessed robotic ability to locate simulated pressure-actuated, low and non-metallic IED trigger switches buried at hidden locations along a route. Finally, Disrupt Challenge assessed the effectiveness of robotic vehicles to disrupt the operation of IEDs and their triggers buried at various depths along a roadway representative of one in theater. The two-week event drew participation from 26 vendors.

OTHER TRANSACTIONS

What Are "Other Transactions"?

"Other Transactions" (OT) refer to contractual instruments that are not standard procurement contracts or standard assistance instruments (grants or cooperative agreements). They may be used to support projects which are not strictly procurement or assistance; in lieu of standard assistance instruments; and, depending on specific statutory authority, for the acquisition of goods and services.

OT's allow agencies and their contracting partners to enter into flexible arrangements tailored to the particular project and needs of the participants. OT's present the parties with a blank page from which to begin negotiations. OT agreements may be fully funded, partially funded (cost-shared), unfunded, and under some statutory authorities funds may be paid to the agency and its appropriations reimbursed. As a general matter, agencies must possess express statutory authority to use OT's.

What Are the Implications of Other Transactions?

- **For program managers:** The great flexibility inherent in OT's is particularly useful in research and development (R&D). The Federal

Acquisition Regulation (FAR) notes that R&D contracts are unlike contracts for supplies and services (FAR 35.002). OT's may be less burdened by the overhead of numerous government regulations that can make government contracting unattractive to many commercial firms. They permit flexibility in crafting intellectual property (IP) provisions because those provisions can be negotiated and can differ from the language typically called for in procurement contracts.

- **For legal:** OT's are generally not subject to laws and regulations specific to procurement and assistance relationships. They are, however, subject to fiscal, criminal, and other laws of general applicability. Some agencies have promulgated regulations governing the use of OT's while others have issued guidance or relied entirely on fundamental statutory authority.
- **For offerors**: The flexibility of OT's can make them attractive to firms and organizations that do not usually participate in government contracting due to the typical overhead burden and "one size fits all" rules. Traditional government contractors may also find exploring new ways of doing business attractive. OT's can also be used to promote cooperative relationships among traditional and non-traditional contractors.

What Are the Benefits of Other Transactions?

Surveys of participants in OT's have characterized their benefits as including streamlining and flexibility. Foremost among these have been the speed and ease of making changes, particularly important in R&D where unexpected results may suggest approaches not foreseen at the initiation of a project. Less time devoted to auditing, flexibility in IP rights and accounting systems are other examples. Other benefits include:

- Performance improvements include a positive influence on team building among participants; team focus on technical aspects of the program; and simplified management and control.
- Schedule reductions have been noted in many projects. These have occurred both before the award and in project execution - aided by a minimization of administrative burden and the flexibility to restructure programs in mid-course resulting in an efficient work

environment. The absence of flow-down provisions can accelerate the performance of commercial firms.

- Cost reductions compared to traditional R&D performance have been noted in OT's. Part of this is attributable to the more timely performance noted in the preceding paragraph. Tradeoffs allowing better use of funds, fewer non-value-added activities, reduced administration and overhead burden and other reasons have also been cited. Cost reductions have been cited for both current performance cost and the cost of future acquisition of the developed product. Studies commissioned by the government have indicated that in DOD acquisition, for example, transaction costs related to mandates unique to the government can add an 18 to 20 percent cost premium. Most if not all of this added cost of doing business can potentially be avoided with OT's.

- OT's have also facilitated the inclusion of non-traditional performers in government programs either on their own or in combination with traditional contractors. Non-traditional firms need not adopt the typical costly government-mandated business and accounting systems and can negotiate IP provisions. In dealing with companies that have established separate divisions for government and commercial work, OT's may allow the government access to the firm's full technical capabilities and not just those of its government division.

What Are the Results or Case Studies to Date?

OT's have been used for a wide variety of science and technology projects, prototype developments, and commercial-style contracting for other purposes. The opinion of most participants and those who have studied the projects in detail has been strongly positive.

FIRE — FAST, INEXPENSIVE, RESTRAINED, ELEGANT

What Is The FIRE Method?

The FIRE (Fast, Inexpensive, Restrained, Elegant) method (formerly FIST – Fast, Inexpensive, Simple, Tiny) provides a heuristic-based decision-making framework designed to foster innovation by establishing constraints on time, money, complexity, and size. The basic premise is that innovation does not have to cost so much, take so long, or be so complicated. The data strongly suggests that the best outcomes are produced by small teams working with short schedules, tight budgets, and deep commitments to simplicity. FIRE orients practitioners toward delivering "affordable systems that are available when needed and effective when used," measuring success in terms of capabilities delivered rather than dollars spent. This is a contrast to the typical approach of treating large price tags and high degrees of complexity as signs of quality, an approach that historically has produced systems which cost more, take longer and do less than promised.

The FIRE method can be applied across the spectrum of decision making, from organizational structure and process design to requirements definition and technical architectures. This approach aims to limit growth in every dimension of the program, to include document length, meeting duration, and team size as well as process complexity, program budget, and delivery schedule. This reduces the risk of program failure and reduces the impact when failures occur.

What Are the Implications of FIRE?

- **For program managers:** Along with heuristics, FIRE equips program managers with concrete principles, tools, and practices to reduce cost, delay, and complexity while maintaining high levels of quality. These field-tested practices reduce the risk of delivering a system that is operationally irrelevant, technologically obsolete, or both. Reducing the cost and schedule also increases the program manager's influence, simplifies accountability, and creates greater opportunity to learn from experience.

- **For legal:** The FIRE method is consistent with the Federal Acquisition Regulation (FAR), which repeatedly encourages restraint and simplicity, and discourages over-engineered solutions. For example, FAR 13.003 emphasizes the use of simplified acquisition procedures, saying "Agencies shall use simplified acquisition procedures to the maximum extent practicable for all purchases of supplies or services not exceeding the simplified acquisition threshold." FAR 15.306(d)(4) recommends the government "suggest to offerors that have exceeded any mandatory minimums…that their proposals would be more competitive if the excesses were removed…"

FAR 35.008 offers similar guidance, explaining that "an award should not be made to obtain capabilities that exceed those needed for successful performance of the work." The modular contracting methods identified in FAR 39.103 are also compatible with FIRE.

- **For offerors**: The FIRE method reduces the two most common barriers to entry that small businesses face when pursuing government contracts: procedural complexity and the sheer size of the government's appetite. FIRE therefore increases openness to (and opportunities for) small business, by reducing both the complexity and scale of programs. FIRE also encourages larger companies to develop skunkworks-style divisions, which Scott Anthony referred to as "corporate garages" in the September 2012 issue of Harvard Business Review. These in-house innovation factories help large companies realize benefits usually available only to smaller, more agile entities.

What Are the Benefits of FIRE?

The FIRE method can provide faster delivery of less expensive solutions, which benefits government customers and taxpayers alike. In addition to being affordable and available, these innovative new capabilities are often first-in-class and/or best-in-class. Implementing simplified procedures opens the door to non-traditional suppliers and smaller entities who were previously unable or unwilling to manage the complexities of government contracting.

From a technical perspective, FIRE can deliver simpler architectures, which means the finished products are easier to debug, more reliable and can be more readily scaled up to larger applications. From an organizational perspective, FIRE can improve and expand the talent pool by increasing opportunity for people to gain experience via smaller, shorter-duration projects.

What Are the Results or Case Studies to Date?

- **NASA's Faster, Better, Cheaper** Missions: These missions in the 1990s demonstrated that it is possible for a government agency to simultaneously improve the cost, schedule, and performance of advanced technical systems. In many cases, program cost dropped by an order of magnitude while technical capability went up an order of magnitude. See "Faster, Better, Cheaper – Revisited" from the March 2010 issue of Defense AT&L magazine for additional analysis and details (http://www.dau.mil/pubscats/atl%20docs/mar-apr10/ward_mar-apr10.pdf).

- **The Navy's Virginia Class submarine program**: This program emphasized speed, thrift, simplicity, and restraint throughout its lifecycle. The results are striking: USS New Hampshire was delivered 8 months early, $54M under budget; the USS Missouri was 9 months early, $72M under budget; and the USS Mississippi was 12 months early, $60M under budget. In fact, the last six submarines were all delivered early.

- **Air Force Institute of Technology** Thesis: A master's degree thesis from the Air Force Institute of Technology (The Effect of Values on System Development Project Outcomes, AFIT/GSE/ENV/09-M08, Maj. Dan Ward) provides a rigorous look at 22 cases from the DoD and NASA. It is available to download from the Defense Technical Information Center: http://www.dtic.mil/dtic/tr/fulltext/u2/a496358.pdf

- **FIRE Book**: *FIRE: How Fast, Inexpensive, Restrained, and Elegant Methods Ignite Innovation* (Dan Ward; Harperbusiness, 2014) documents further results and provides an introduction to the FIRE tools, practices, and principles.

AGILE METHODS

What Are Agile Methods?

Agile is not one specific method; Agile is both a philosophy and an umbrella term for a collection of methods or approaches that share certain common characteristics. The Agile philosophy is embodied in the 4 tenets of the Agile Manifesto and the 12 associated principles. Various Agile methods (e.g., Scrum, eXtreme Programming (XP), Adaptive Software Development, etc.) have been and continue to be created that instantiate the tenets and principles. The first and second elements are intentionally general and vague (tenets and principles). The third element, Agile methods, is more concrete in that each specifies practices to be performed. There are many Agile methods and each emphasizes different aspects of Agile. For example, the Agile Scrum method has a heavy software management emphasis (e.g. daily team meetings and a sprint-based lifecycle). Another example is XP that emphasizes the technical aspects of Agile (e.g., pair programming and continuous integration). When adopting Agile, organizations should select the method(s) that most closely aligns with its goals (e.g., effective small team leadership practices, and increase efficiency and reduce waste).

People generally agree on three key elements of Agile stated above. However, there is no universally accepted formal definition for Agile. One informal definition from an Agile practitioner is: "Agile is an iterative and incremental (evolutionary) approach to software development which is performed in a highly collaborative manner by self-organizing teams within an effective governance framework, with 'just enough' ceremony, that produces high quality solutions, in a cost effective and timely manner which meets the changing needs of its stakeholders."

What Are the Implications of Agile Methods?

- **For program managers:** There are two sets of implications – those for adopting and those for practicing agile methods. The management role in an Agile program takes on some added dimensions. Program managers (both acquiring and executing) not only have to be leaders, but they also need to be coaches, expeditors, and champions. If not personally performing these roles, they will need someone within their organizations responsible for them. However, adoption of any new acquisition lifecycle requires a change in the prevailing culture. Adopting Agile is not any different. There are differences in perspective on many elements such as organization structure, rewards system, communications, decision-making, and staffing model. To meet the challenges of adopting Agile, a program management office (PMO) can take specific actions. Terminology will need to be learned or relearned if terms have different meanings when using Agile. In order to employ any Agile concept, the government organization will need to plan for it, train for it, anticipate changes in the environment and business model, and apply hard work to make the changes a reality. Once adopted, the transparent nature of the Agile approach provides continuous and immediate insight into the state of the project.

- **For Legal:** The White House recently released two documents, the TechFAR Handbook and Digital Services Playbook, which document the best processes and practices, including Agile, to advance smarter IT delivery in the government. The TechFAR Handbook, in particular, highlights the flexibilities in the Federal Acquisition Regulation that support the use of contractors for Agile software development. The goal is for agency stakeholders to be trained on and use this guidance, which will include relevant authorities, practice tips, case studies, and sample language from successful contracts for Agile software development.

  In addition, Section 804 of the National Defense Authorization Act (NDAA) of 2010 states a new acquisition process is required for information technology systems. "The acquisition process developed and implemented pursuant to this subsection shall, to the extent determined appropriate by the Secretary— (1) be based on the recommendations in chapter 6 of the March 2009 report of the Defense Science Board Task Force on Department of Defense Policies and Procedures for the Acquisition of Information Technology; and (2) be designed to include—

  (A) early and continual involvement of the user;

  (B) multiple, rapidly executed increments or releases of capability;

  (C) early, successive prototyping to support an evolutionary approach; and

  (D) a modular, open-systems approach."

The FAR also provides some sections that may be useful. FAR 16.3, Cost Reimbursement, LOE-Term FAR 16.306(d)(2) and indefinite delivery FAR 16.5 provide potential implementation ideas.

For offerors: Agile provides contractors an alternative approach to developing software based on the software practitioner's perspective. Agile methods provide transparency for both internal contractor management and government customers. Constant collaboration between the contractors and the government personnel increases the understanding of the requirements which potentially results in a product better suited to the needs of the end users.

What Are the Benefits of Agile Methods?

Agile methods show greater promise in enabling organizations to adjust to changing requirements and rapidly field software as compared to other development approaches such as the waterfall approach. In contrast to waterfall-based projects, Agile seeks to deliver small but functioning software in increments that eventually build up to the full desired capability. In this manner, users can begin to interact with the software system earlier. Users receive some minimal capability early rather than waiting until the end of the entire waterfall life cycle to receive any working software. This reduces lifecycle costs by eliminating the development of unnecessary and unwanted features. Additional benefits seen from using Agile Methods include:

- early insight by the users into the actual design and implementation of the solution
- early and ongoing insight by the developers into user behavior, leading to more usable applications
- the ability to change requirements and priorities throughout the life cycle
- opportunities to "fail fast" and make timely adjustments if the early solution ideas turn out to be flawed, little time or money is spent before that learning occurs, and redirection can be implemented
- because each iteration or sprint involves unit testing and acceptance testing, bugs are revealed and addressed earlier in the process
- an explicit framework for discussing priorities and tradeoffs, leading to more accurate assessments of the state of the project at any given time
- an explicit understanding on the part of the development and acquiring organizations that the requirements are expected to evolve and are a natural part of software development and ensuring value is delivered to the customer

What Are the Results or Case Studies to Date?

Many of the results and case studies to date are anecdotal. However, there are some studies available.

- **GAO report**. GAO-12-681: Effective Practices and Federal Challenges in Applying Agile Methods. This report provides experiences in 5 agencies. The authors found that 10 of 32 Agile practices identified for consideration were being used and deemed effective. They also noted 14 challenges identified reflecting on the need to transition to Agile.
- **Patriot Excalibur (PEX)**. PEX has been using agile methods for software development for over a decade. The program has successfully delivered and evolved a squadron support system that has been voluntarily adopted by more than 600 organizations. The development staff has grown from 10 to 100 and the program has a highly engaged user community that sets requirements and direction for the next version of the software. It was named one of the five top software projects by CrossTalk magazine in 2004.
- **National Geospatial-Intelligence Agency (NGA)**. The agency's enterprise-wide adoption of Agile was given at the AFEI/SEI Agile for Government Summit on November 20, 2013. "NGA is shaping a cultural shift and adopting agile principles for the NGA enterprise."

CHARTS: AN OVERVIEW OF THE DIFFERENT INNOVATION MODELS

The two charts below are designed to provide the various offices involved in an acquisition an overview of how each innovative model can be used, depending on the goal and needs of the agency.

Goal	Rapid Technology Prototyping	Staged Contracts	Milestone-Based Competitions	Incentive Prizes	Challenge Based Acquisitions
Business Participation					
Attract innovative small businesses	✓	✓	✓	✓	✓
Attract businesses or organization new to government contracting	✓	✓	✓	✓	✓
Mission Requirements					
Develop complex, incremental systems					
Develop discrete areas or modules for complex, incremental systems	✓	✓	✓	✓	✓
Determine if there are any solutions to a known problem	✓	✓	✓	✓	✓
Make testing less expensive	✓	✓	✓	✓	✓
Encourage industry investment first				✓	✓
Obtain a concept paper before buying a prototype		✓			
Provide for follow-on contracting for production			✓		
Obtain short proposals (less than 10 pages) or prototypes	✓	✓		✓	✓
Use special authority outside the FAR for competition				✓	
Prototype Requirements					
Test pre-existing prototypes before buying		✓		✓	✓
Build low cost prototype	✓			✓	
Test prototypes in relevant demonstration scenario	✓	✓	✓	✓	✓
Solicitation Type					
Use a standard solicitation such as an RFP for a well-defined, multi-component problem		✓	✓		✓
Use an R&D type solicitation such as a BAA to provide objectives but not specifications	✓	✓	✓	✓	✓
Funding Type					
Use firm fixed type pricing funding	✓	✓	✓	✓	✓
Utilize milestone based payments		✓	✓	✓	✓
Program Office					
Attract innovative small businesses	✓	✓	✓	✓	✓
Attract businesses new to contracting	✓	✓	✓	✓	✓
Develop complex, incremental systems					
Develop discrete modules for complex, incremental systems	✓	✓	✓	✓	✓

(Continued)

Goal	Rapid Technology Prototyping	Staged Contracts	Milestone-Based Competitions	Incentive Prizes	Challenge Based Acquisitions
Determine if there are solutions to a known problem	✓	✓	✓	✓	✓
Make testing less expensive	✓	✓	✓	✓	✓
Encourage industry investment first				✓	✓
Obtain a concept paper before buying a prototype		✓			
Obtain short proposals (<10 pages) or prototypes	✓	✓		✓	✓
Test pre-existing prototypes before buying		✓		✓	✓
Build low cost prototype	✓			✓	
Test prototypes in relevant demonstration scenario	✓	✓	✓	✓	✓
Procurement Office					
Use a standard solicitation such as an RFP for a well-defined, multi-component problem		✓	✓		✓
Use an R&D type solicitation such as a BAA to provide objectives but not specifications	✓	✓	✓	✓	✓
Provide for follow-on contracting for production			✓		
Use firm fixed type pricing funding	✓	✓	✓	✓	✓
Utilize milestone based payments		✓	✓	✓	✓
Legal					
Use special authority outside the FAR				✓	
Use FAR authority	✓	✓	✓		✓

RAPID TECHNOLOGY PROTOTYPING: FINDING THE RIGHT INNOVATION FROM SMALL BUSINESSES

Overview

To find the right innovations for an agency, the government needs the ability to rapidly and cheaply assess new technologies. One way to accomplish this is through multiple, small, fast, and cheap acquisitions that have the contractor develop prototypes applying the new technology to relevant demonstration scenarios. This allows the agency to try out functional research prototypes to assess the viability of the technology prior to a substantial government investment. The effectiveness of the technology then allows decisions regarding additional investment of government resources to be results-driven and significantly reduces the cost, schedule, and technology risks for any subsequent work. This module outlines some of the considerations in using these innovative contracting models.

Manage Failure

Substantial gains in innovation are often accompanied by substantial trial and error on big ideas. Thus, in R&D contracting one may need to accept, and even embrace the potential of failure as the mark of innovative thinking. Innovative thinking can thrive in a space that allows for failure in order to leap ahead.

Therefore, most prototyping attempts will not result in a follow-on project to move the prototype into production. Thus, the key to this program is to manage failure. A realistic expectation for success rates in terms of establishing follow-on projects is only 10% to 30%. Although most projects will end in failure, these failures are key to the success of the program and a recognized component of R&D contracting.

- **Fail Early.** All initial prototype projects should be scheduled for three to six months with a hard deadline to produce a working, demonstrable prototype at the end. If the company cannot deliver a working prototype within this timeframe, then the project stops. Although draconian, this approach allows limited government resources to effectively assess a large number of possibilities rapidly and cheaply to identify the ones which are the most viable. Most ideas will not work out, but the few that succeed make the overall effort worthwhile.

- **Fail Cheaply.** The initial three to six month prototype projects should be done as Firm Fixed Price contracts which are executed in the company's own facilities. This eliminates cost risk to the government and emphasizes that the project is a test to see if they can deliver a working prototype on schedule and budget. Using the company's own facility eliminates extra costs or delays associated with using a government facility for the development work. A contract value between $50,000 and $100,000 is adequate for a prototype project of this duration. Any additional government investment should only be done after there is definite and objective proof the technology is working as advertised to minimize technical risks incurred by the government. However, the company should be allowed to contribute its own Internal Research and Development (IR&D) funding to the project to jointly fund this initial effort, if so desired.

- **Fail Often.** If a high percentage of the initial projects are succeeding and producing follow-on projects, then it is likely that the initial projects are focusing more on existing and proven technologies instead of pursuing innovative and potentially breakthrough new technologies. If the success rate for establishing follow-on projects for innovative technologies is between 10% and 30%, the projects that are successful are likely to represent valuable new capabilities. Additionally, important lessons could be learned from the non-successful projects to help guide the agency's future technology directions. This is why it is important to try as many initial projects as possible given the resource constraints instead of investing a great deal of resources in just a few initial projects.

- **Fail Smartly.** Although most of these initial projects are expected to fail, they should not fail due to a lack of government involvement or due to some other confounding variable. Every project should be given the best chance to succeed. The agency can derive lessons learned from each failure and use them to improve the overall program.

Using This Innovative Model

The main objective is to design the acquisition approach and the request for proposal (RFP) to result in a large number of good proposals describing innovative technologies, ideas, and approaches relevant to the agency's requirements. A second, but equally important, objective is to design the RFP so it expedites the overall acquisition process by designing out or mitigating any areas or issues that could cause delays to the acquisition process or the resulting prototype development projects. The Broad Agency Announcement (BAA) mechanism can serve as the basis of the acquisition effort.

Identifying the Problems/Requirements

The problems/requirements included in the RFP need to be thought of as "bait" to attract and challenge companies to focus on solutions for these problems. Problems can be very specific with a defined result required (e.g., develop a new algorithm that can solve A, B and C with a run time under Y minutes on X amount of data on a computer with no more than Z processors). Or the problems can be very high level (e.g., looking for new types of analytics that can run effectively on large scale data). The key to the problems is to provide enough background information so a company can make an intelligent assessment about what would be required and desired in a solution. Additionally, even if a company decides to not submit a proposal, the background information provided about the problems/requirements can start to educate industry on the agency's requirements, which assists companies to submit more relevant proposals in the future. In all cases, regardless of whether a problem is specific or general, submission of proposals should not be limited to only the problems/requirements specified in the RFP. There should always be an option for the company to submit a proposal under their own category in case there is relevant innovation in an area of which the agency is unaware.

The expectations for problems/requirements should also be sensitive to the time limits of prototype development and focus on what can realistically be achieved in the allowed timeframe. If a problem/requirement implies a much larger problem, then the problem/requirement can focus on prototyping proofs of concept to illustrate the viability of key components of the solution instead of focusing on prototyping the complete, but much larger, solution.

Another type of information very useful to companies when crafting their response is a description of approaches or technologies that the agency is not interested in. The "Not Interested In" list could be common approaches which have been tried so often that there is very little value in trying them again.

This list could also include approaches the agency knows will not work effectively based on internal research. The reasons the agency is not interested do not have to be included with the description of the "Not Interested In" approach/technology.

If specific requirements or constraints exist for a particular problem and its potential solutions, this information should also be included in the problem description. Some common specific constraints are: minimum performance requirements, the use of certain software or platforms, minimum data amounts, the use of a particular set of test data, etc.

Engaging the Future End Users
Potential end users should be engaged as early as possible, and the end users should be the main participants in identifying the problems/requirements. End users should be identified from among the subject matter experts and

power users in an office because they are most likely to truly understand where the gaps exist in their technologies and what new capabilities are needed to take their work to the next level. When an office contributes some of its own funding to support the acquisition effort, the office is much more likely to support continued engagement by the end users.

Constraining the Solution Space

While it is important to not constrain the ideas, it is very important to constrain the support technologies used to implement the prototype to give each technology its best chance of being integrated into existing systems if the technology proves successful. Unlike the private sector, the reality of many government systems is they are not going to undergo any large scale replacement and, instead, need to evolve in place to incorporate new technologies and capabilities. This makes it necessary to constrain the solution space so potential new capabilities are designed to facilitate integration with existing systems. For example, if most existing systems at an agency use Linux servers and Windows clients, then this type of architecture should be a requirement for potential new capabilities. If the potential capability does not have the flexibility to use the specified architecture, it likely will not be able to be used regardless of its potential benefit. Thus, it is best to discover this issue early. Some good constraints to consider are:

- A preference for using Open Source software where suitable software is available to minimize licensing costs
- No reliance or dependency on proprietary data formats or data storage mechanisms
- Web-enabled GUIs and user facing applications
- Software developed using a common language such as C, C++, or Java
- Use of specific standards or protocols

Solutions based on commercial products are generally less successful than solutions based on open technologies because commercial products may be less cutting-edge and innovative due to the amount of time it takes to bring a commercial product to market. Additionally, commercial products generally are associated with significant licensing fees that can be unrealistic for widespread government usage.

Identifying Participants

The goal is to have the RFP reach as many suitable companies as possible including a significant number of companies that may be new to Federal contracting. The use of this model, with its shortened timeframe of producing a prototype in 6 months or less, and at a dollar value under the simplified acquisition threshold, should encourage participation by entrepreneurs and innovative small businesses.

However, recognize that if the agency decides to go into production of the prototype, some of the companies may lack adequate cash flow management or have difficulties adjusting to the government's sometimes lengthy payment schedule, complex Federal Acquisition Regulation (FAR) and Defense Federal Acquisition Regulation (DFAR) contract clauses, and lengthy government acquisition cycles. Therefore, it may be beneficial to prescreen companies for interest using a market survey or some other advance notice of the upcoming acquisition to ensure they understand the requirements of a Federal acquisition.

Developing the RFP

There are two goals for the RFP: (1) Design the RFP to eliminate as many delays and obstacles as possible and automatically mitigate what cannot be eliminated; and (2) Have the proposals responding to the RFP include sufficient information to support comprehensive evaluations and allow the proposal to serve as the Statement of Work (SOW) for any resulting contracts. If the resulting proposals are complete, comprehensive, and contain all information necessary to support proposal evaluation and contract award, the acquisition process can be expedited because the Contracting Officer will not have to hold discussions with the company to resolve areas which are unclear or are contrary to the government's requirements. If the resulting proposal is sufficiently complete, it can serve as the SOW for any resulting contract which will also expedite the acquisition process.

The delays and obstacles encountered when awarding a contract for technical work will be specific to each agency, but here are some common issues that can be set forth in the RFP:

1. *IT Governance* – If an agency has IT Governance requirements dictating or forbidding the use of specific hardware or software, this information should be included in the RFP as requirements for all

resulting projects. For example, many agencies are standardized on the use of the Windows operating system for client applications and on the use of the Linux operating system for back end server applications. If this is the case, then this information should be a requirement in the RFP. If there are two possible technical options for supporting potential solutions and additional approvals are required for one option but not the other option, consider limiting the company's IT choices for their prototype to the option that does not require the additional approvals.

2. *Security* – Different agencies have different security requirements for companies performing work. If there are options or approaches that require less approval than other options or approaches, to expedite the process, it may be beneficial to make the option requiring less approval mandatory if it will not unduly constrain the resulting prototype development effort. Security requirements and restrictions can always be revisited for successful prototypes when planning for longer term follow-on work.

3. *Intellectual Property and Government Rights* – The RFP needs to clearly state the conditions that will apply to all Intellectual Property developed under any contracts resulting from the project and whether the FAR/DFAR (or other agency specific) clauses regarding intellectual property will apply. Additionally, the RFP should state the minimum level of rights the agency is willing to accept, for example, Government Purpose rights, for all work developed under resulting contracts. Companies should also be informed in the RFP that offering to provide the prototype with rights less than the minimum level the agency is willing to accept may negatively impact their proposal evaluation.

4. *Payments* – Although contracts are likely to be firm fixed price, most efforts will involve incremental payments. The RFP should identify the payment schedule and tie each payment into a specific deliverable, for example, invoice #1 corresponds to the delivery of monthly status report #1. The company can then propose the amount for each scheduled payment. Having all companies follow the same payment schedule and identifying the payment amounts up front eliminates a common time-consuming item for Contracting Officer discussions with the company and simplifies the management of multiple projects after award.

5. *Deliverables* – The RFP needs to clearly define what deliverables are associated with any resulting contracts. If there are requirements for a deliverable that are beyond what is described in the Data Item Description (DID) for that deliverable, these additional requirements need to be clearly noted in the RFP. The minimum technical deliverables should be: 1) written monthly status reports; 2) a prototype and a prototype demonstration; and 3) delivery of all source code, documentation, licenses, and other materials needed to allow the government to install and run the prototype on the agency's hardware in a government facility for a year to fully assess the prototype.

6. *Automatic Disqualification* – The RFP should also specifically state the conditions that would automatically disqualify a proposal from consideration. This will save both the agency and the company a great deal of time and should mostly eliminate the receipt of non-compliant proposals. Some common conditions that could cause an automatic disqualification are: 1) proposing a cost exceeding the amount allowed by the government; 2) proposing a schedule that exceeds the time allotted by the government; 3) not adhering to the government's requirements in the RFP when writing the proposal; and 4) proposing to deliver something other than a prototype (e.g., a requirements document, a study).

7. *Test Data* – A significant challenge in developing rapid prototypes is obtaining a sufficient amount of suitable test data to make the prototype's operations relevant to the larger agency requirements. Where possible, the RFP should identify publically available collections of test data consistent with the agency's own data as well as describe collections of government test data that could be provided to companies upon contract award.

8. *Proposal Content and Format*– If the RFP provides specific instructions on the content and format of the proposals, it will expedite evaluation of the proposals and make it more likely that companies will include all necessary and relevant information in their proposals. For example, the RFP could request the proposal to include the following content in the Technical proposal:

   a. Executive Summary – Intended to provide an overview of the salient features of the entire proposal.

   b. State-of-the-Art – A description of the current state-of-the-art concerning the proposed technology/approach, a discussion of comparable products, technologies and/or approaches similar to what the company is proposing, and an explanation of why what the company is proposing is well beyond the current state-of-the-art.

c. Description of the Prototype – A discussion of the idea being addressed by the prototype, identification of the key challenges, description of the proposed solution, a detailed research plan and technical approach to implement the functional prototype within the specified timeframe, and identification of the personnel and other resources available for the work.

d. Facilities, Software Frameworks/Data Sets and GFI – A description of the facilities the company has available to use for this work and identification of any equipment that needs to be purchased to support this effort. Any hardware, software, data, or documentation items the company wants to request from the government to support this effort need to be identified in the proposal so potential delays in providing these items to the company can be factored into the proposal evaluation.

e. Technical Data or Computer Software – Identification of all technical data or computer software that will be furnished to the government and the rights that will be provided to the government for each item.

f. Sub-Contracts or Relevant Collaborations – A description of any proposed sub-contracts or relevant collaborations planned or already in place with industry, government organizations, universities, or other institutions.

g. Other Parties – Identification of other parties to whom the proposal has been or will be sent.

h. Deliverables – A detailed description of all deliverables to be provided to the government as a result of the work and in accordance with the requirements in the Contract Data Requirements List.

i. Past Performance in similar R&D work.

j. Relevant Experience of Company and/or Key Personnel in the area being proposed.

The RFP should also specify page limits for the Technical and Management proposals. For short, rapid prototyping efforts, a 15-page Technical Proposal and a 5-page Management Proposal should be sufficient.

This length is sufficient to provide a comprehensive description of the work, and it can still support relatively rapid proposal evaluations.

Evaluating Proposals and Selecting for Award

The proposal evaluation plan should reserve the right to fund all, some, or none of the proposals received under the BAA solicitation in order to retain the greatest flexibility for the government. A key point to make in the proposal evaluation plan is that the awards will be done in an effort to achieve a balanced program providing the best value to the government. Focusing on a balanced program will permit the government to consider factors other than absolute technical scores or lowest cost in making the selections so the government can select a mix of awards which provides the biggest benefit to the government. The wording listed below describes one way this right can be reserved in the RFP:

> "The Government reserves the right to shift funding across problem and topic tracks and/or add additional funding based on the quality of the proposals. Award(s) resulting from this BAA will be made to the responsible offerors whose offers, conforming to the BAA, represent in aggregate the greatest potential for contributing to the Government's current technical research needs as described in the BAA. The Government may select proposals for award that have lower technical or overall ratings if it is determined that the mix of topics represented by the awarded proposals represents the best value to the Government by providing a balanced program."

The proposal evaluation criteria should be simple and straightforward. Three evaluation criteria that work effectively for small, rapid prototyping projects are:

1. Overall Technical Merit
   a. Scientific and technical merit
   b. Innovativeness and uniqueness
   c. Viability and practicality of technical approach d. Prototype capabilities
2. Potential Contribution and Relevance to the Mission
   a. Relevance and importance
   b. Applicability and validity
   c. Usefulness and effectiveness
3. Cost and Schedule Realism

    a.   Schedule feasibility
    b.   Risk Management
    c.   Cost Realism

A two phase evaluation process also works well for small, rapid prototyping projects. Phase 1 consists of up to three reviewers independently evaluating and rating each proposal. If many proposals are received or if different proposals require different technical expertise, then different reviewers could be assigned to each proposal so the same three people do not have to evaluate each proposal. In Phase 2, a technical peer review is conducted by a small group of stakeholders to consider the evaluation information provided by the three independent reviewers and determine the specific proposals to be recommended for award that represent the best value to the government by producing a balanced program.

Executing the Award

The main objective in executing the awarded contracts is to produce demonstrable prototypes of the new technologies that are as relevant as possible to the government's requirements thereby allowing informed, results-based decisions to be made regarding any follow-on work and additional investment to turn the prototypes in actual mission capabilities. Additionally, if the company is able to deliver the prototype on schedule and budget and if the prototype has the capabilities and features stipulated in the original proposal, this is a good indication that the company is likely to be successful on any subsequent work.

Involving End Users

It is critical for end users to be involved with oversight of the technology aspects of each project, but it is equally important that the technical end users do not have to spend their limited and valuable time on the administrative aspects of the project, especially when most of the projects will not continue into follow-on work and will just stop at the end of the contract's period of performance. If many of the issues that could cause delays or obstacles to execution are designed out of the program from the beginning, then one person can easily handle the administrative duties for multiple awardees, leaving the technical end users to solely focus on the technical aspects of the work. Offices that have a need for the capabilities potentially offered by the technology and offices that would have to be involved in implementing the prototype into production environments are good sources for technical end users to participate in technical discussions with the company after contract execution.

Managing Risk and Establishing Expectations

The key to effectively managing small, rapid prototyping projects is to allow the company to manage all execution risk and avoid any dependencies on the government for information, approvals, or other items. The government's expectations for the company should be defined and clearly articulated up front so the company knows what to expect in terms of meetings and teleconferences, prototype demonstrations, and level and amount of technical guidance and advice that will be provided. Very frequent interactions between the company and government personnel, such as participation of government personnel in the company's daily technical meetings, should be avoided to minimize adding too much government bias to the effort and avoid shifting additional risk onto the government.

Providing Technical Guidance and Advice

That said, there should be regular opportunities during the execution of the project for the Government's technical end users to ask questions of the company about the work being done and for the company to ask the technical end users questions about requirements, system environments, demonstration scenarios, relevant use cases, etc. Teleconferences can easily take the place of face-to- face meetings, especially where time or location considerations apply to the personnel participating in these meetings. The objective is to provide the company with sufficient information about the government's needs so that the company can develop the most relevant prototype possible given the cost and schedule constraints.

Demonstrating and Testing Prototypes

A prototype demonstration at the end of the contract provides an effective assessment of the work that has been done and should clearly illustrate how the technology could potentially be applied to mission requirements. The technical end users should assist the company in defining relevant use cases and crafting the demonstrations scenarios so the prototype illustrates relevant operational situations as much as possible. Seeing the technology function under pseudo-operational situations should allow results-based decisions to be made regarding the viability and relevance of the technology.

The demonstration of a functional research prototype also serves to verify that the work was actually done and something was built.

Pursuing Follow-on Work

Prototypes selected for follow-on work should be transferred to the standard acquisition processes supporting the development of mission systems. Technical end users who participated in the execution phase of the project are likely candidates for sponsoring the follow-on work. The prototype itself may serve as justification for a sole source follow-on contract for the company.

Companies with prototypes that are not considered for follow-on work should be notified and provided with constructive feedback as to why their prototype was not selected for follow-on work so the company can improve its efforts in the future.

Rapid Technology Successes

Rapid technology prototyping has been used by the Department of Defense with respect to 3D mapping prototypes of urban terrain, for radio detection finder systems, and for sensor mechanisms that detect improvised explosive devices and provide warnings to ground forces.

Conclusion

The Rapid Technology Prototyping model described in this paper can be effective at rapidly and cheaply assessing many potential new technologies to identify the viable options for meeting an agency's particular requirements. This approach, which uses the BAA acquisition method, can easily be tailored and customized to meet the specific requirements and constraints of different government agencies. Among the innovative contracting models, Rapid Technology Prototyping contracts can uniquely:

- Encourage small businesses to partner with others (including other small businesses or academia) to transform basic research developments into applied research that could potentially be used to address the government's requirements.
- Facilitate knowledge transfer from the government to small businesses to better enable the small business to support the government's requirements.

- Effectively utilize limited government resources (time and money) to rapidly assess many technologies and make results-based decisions regarding further investment.

STAGED CONTRACTS: IDENTIFYING SCALABLE INNOVATIONS FOR TAILORED GOVERNMENT SOLUTIONS

Overview

Not all innovation is relevant to a particular government agency, and many innovations cannot be effectively used to meet an agency's particular requirements. Staged contracts can allow government agencies to rapidly funnel the landscape of promising private sector technologies into rigorously evaluated pilots to inform potential agency-wide deployment. Quickly filtering the submissions allows the government to identify the most promising technologies with strong potential for wide impact, and invite these applicants to submit a full proposal for subsequent pilot testing. The evaluation of the technology allows decisions regarding additional investment of government resources to be results- driven and significantly reduces the cost, time, and technology risks for subsequent scale-up work.

The Department of Veterans Affairs Innovation Initiative (VAi2) Industry Innovation Competition illustrates the promise of staged contracts. The VAi2 Competition did not award contracts for the full 12-24 month implementation until two previous stages of paper evaluations had been completed: initial concept papers followed by invitation-only full proposals. The VAi2 Broad Agency Announcement (BAA) was issued under Federal Acquisition Regulation (FAR) Parts 35.016 and 6.102(d)(2)(i), which provide for the competitive selection of proposals submitted in response to a BAA. The VAi2 competition has awarded no fewer than 135 solutions worth $102.5 million, fielded solutions in eight topic areas, received over 20,000 ideas from 600 industry offerors, and collaborated with over 100 subject matter experts.

The VAi2 Competition staged contracts followed a three-phase process consisting of an eight-page concept paper, 50-page invite-only full proposal, and 1-2 year pilot evaluation. In general, staged contracts work as follows:

1. *Announce:* agencies release a broad solicitation for contractors to submit short concept papers communicating the essence of their proposed technologies.
2. *Study:* agencies invite promising offerors to submit detailed full proposals with both technical and cost/price components.
3. *Evaluate:* agencies evaluate selected full proposals in 1-2 year pilots, during which there is ample opportunity for offerors to communicate with end users and refine their technology.
4. *Deploy:* agencies decide to deploy, terminate, or further evaluate pilots.

The Innovation Funnel: VAi2 Competition

Reducing the burdens of responding to government contracts is imperative for agencies to attract small business innovation. Staged contracts, by forgoing the extensive requirements of traditional acquisition processes in favor of short concept papers, let agencies sample the diverse technology landscape for potential solutions. These concept papers allow BAA respondents to communicate the essence of their proposal without expending undue time and effort. In this way, staged contracts reduce administrative burden for both offerors and agencies. Furthermore, staged contracts can solicit proposals in multiple topic areas. The 2012 VAi2 BAA hosted topic areas ranging from "Women's Health: Maternity Tracker" to "Prevention and Treatment of Pressure Ulcers" to "Mobile Technology and Applications for Veteran Benefits."

Wide Solicitation

Staged contracts offer agencies a tool to solicit proposals widely across the private sector—from established contractors to entrepreneurs—and rapidly assess them. For example, the VAi2 competition attracted a 50-50 mix of established and first-time government contractors. Staged contracts require offerors to submit only an initial summary slide and eight page concept paper instead of the hundreds of pages expected in traditional acquisition processes. This dramatic decrease in the burden of doing business with government may better ensure that successful offerors' core competencies lie not in proposal drafting but in delivering technology solutions. Moreover, the initial solicitation encourages small business participation with its simplicity—the VAi2 BAA spans only 22 pages, including appendices and references. The solicitation's open-ended nature emphasizes contractor creativity. However, these same qualities require agencies to ensure that the procurement office assists applicants and provides adequate government engagement. In summary, leveling the barrier to do business with government from a 300+ page RFP response to an eight-page concept paper promises to increase and diversify the participation of small businesses and other innovators.

Focused Validation

Staged contracts' extensive evaluative process ensures that solutions are customized to meet the specific requirements of the government agency. From solicitation to pilot completion, offerors' solutions are vetted during at least three dedicated evaluation periods: concept paper review, full proposal review, and pilot evaluation. Solutions undergoing pilot evaluations are not guaranteed agency-wide scale-up: unsatisfactory pilots can warrant further development, project termination, or user deployment. The hands-on, real-time implementation of pilots and frequent, informal communications with end users during the period of performance provides offerors invaluable feedback to tailor their solutions more precisely to government requirements.

Challenges & Limitations

The process of rapidly funneling solutions into rigorously evaluated pilots does present several challenges. First, agencies must be thoughtful in articulating the problem statement, its scope, and the types of solutions sought. Subject matter experts may be inclined to focus the problem statement too narrowly, excluding potential innovative solutions. Contract officers must be comfortable embracing the fact that the government does not know what the solution looks like and must craft the problem statement accordingly to harness open-ended innovation. Second, agencies must acknowledge and prepare for the uncertainty of contract funding, especially because each contract extends across two to three years. Third, staged contract pilot sites may experience difficulties handling unforeseen timing issues, integrating prototype technologies within existing systems, and receiving buy-in from pilot staff. Finally, the requirements for full and open competition in the Competition in Contracting Act of 1984 may pose obstacles for agencies seeking to transition pilots into sole source follow-on contracts. Despite these challenges, the VAi2 Competition has demonstrated that the technology pilots themselves can provide agencies significant value.

There are limitations to the applicability of staged contracts. As staged contracts are designed to rigorously implement and evaluate ideas—either novel or established in the private sector—within a short timeframe, these contracts may not be optimal for the engineering of complex, incremental systems on the one hand, or for the rapid development of cutting-edge prototypes on the other hand (see the previous chapter for a different contracting model for rapid prototyping).

Using This Innovative Model

The main objective using a staged contracting model is to design the acquisition approach and the RFP to result in a large number of high-quality proposals describing innovative technologies, ideas, and approaches relevant to the agency's requirements. A second, but equally important, objective is to design the RFP so that it expedites the overall acquisition process by "designing out" or mitigating any areas or issues that could cause delays to the acquisition process or the resulting prototype development projects. The BAA mechanism can serve as the basis of the acquisition effort.

Identifying the Problems/Requirements

The problems/requirements included in the BAA need to be thought of as "bait" to attract and challenge companies to focus on solutions for these problems. The key to the problems is to provide enough background information so a company can make an intelligent assessment about what would be required and desired in a solution. Agencies must spend considerable time engaging end users to define problems adequately, while resisting the temptation to prescribe solution requirements. Additionally, even if a company decides to not submit a proposal, the background information provided about the problems/requirements can start to educate industry on the agency's requirements, which assists companies to submit more relevant proposals in the future.

It may be helpful to choose initial areas of interest adjacent to ongoing high-complexity, high-centrality, and high-visibility agency initiatives. Such initiatives will likely have well-defined challenges and subject matter experts the BAA could draw from. Additionally, the high visibility of the initiative may attract increased private sector interest for the BAA. Despite these preparations, challenges in appropriately scoping and defining the problems may arise. For example, organizers of the inaugural VAi2 Industry Innovation Competition solicited proposals in the area of telehealth and required 350-page submissions. Seeing that the scope was too broad and initial dive too deep, organizers requested 28-page concept papers in the area of teleaudiology the second year, before instituting the current two-phase process consisting of an eight-page concept paper and 50-page technical proposal.

If specific requirements or constraints exist for a particular problem and its potential solutions, this information should also be included in the problem description. Some common specific constraints are: minimum performance requirements, the use of certain software or platforms, minimum data amounts, the use of a particular set of test data, etc.

Engaging the Future End Users

Potential agency end users should be engaged as early as possible, and these end users should be major participants in identifying the problems/ requirements. End users should be identified from among the subject matter experts and "power users" in an office because they are most likely to truly understand where the gaps exist in their technologies and what new capabilities are needed to take their work to the next level. When an office contributes some of its own funding to support the acquisition effort, the office is much more likely to support continued engagement by the end users.

Engaging with potential end users early could lead to a clearer articulation of agency areas of interest for innovative technologies in the BAA, which is particularly important should the BAA contain multiple areas of interest. For example, the VAi2 BAA prioritized dialogue with end users and subject matter experts to craft detailed one-pagers for each topic area, providing background on the problem (e.g. scope and impact) and explicitly listing what features the VA was interested in.

Constraining the Solution Space

While it is important not to define the problem statement too narrowly, at the same time it is critical to constrain the support technologies used to implement the prototype, in order to give each technology its best chance of being integrated into existing systems if the technology proves successful. The reality of many government systems is they are not going to undergo large-scale replacement and, instead, need to evolve in place to incorporate new technologies and capabilities. This makes it necessary to constrain the solution space so potential new capabilities are designed to facilitate integration with existing systems. For example, if most existing systems at an agency use Linux servers and Windows clients, then this type of architecture should be a requirement for potential new capabilities. If the potential capability does not have the flexibility to use the specified architecture, it likely will not be able to be used regardless of its potential benefit. Thus, it is best to discover this issue early. Some important constraints to consider are:

- A preference for using Open Source software where suitable software is available to minimize licensing costs
- No reliance or dependency on proprietary data formats or data storage mechanisms
- Web-enabled GUIs and user facing applications
- Software developed using a common language such as C, C++, or Java
- Use of specific standards or protocols

Solutions based on commercial products are generally less successful than solutions based on open technologies; commercial products may be less cutting-edge, due to the amount of time it takes to bring a commercial product to market. Additionally, commercial products generally are associated with significant licensing fees that can be unrealistic for widespread government usage.

In addition, requiring concept papers to identify themselves as Development Proposals vs. Field Test Proposals can be helpful in signaling to agencies the technology's maturity. This information informs appropriate expectations and focus for the technical review committee and pilot managers regarding implementation readiness, evaluation, and scale-up potential. For example, pilot managers may prioritize repeatability and rigorous testing for Field Test Proposals, in contrast to achieving a working prototype for Development Proposals. Distinguishing proposals may also inform the selection of appropriate pilot sites. For example, Development Projects may not be well-suited for centralized, fast- paced pilot sites as failure risks may interrupt integral agency services. To coordinate agency efforts, both proposal types should be kept on consistent timelines, such as a 12-24 month period for pilot implementation and evaluation.

The VAi2 BAA provided the following definitions for Development Proposals and Field Test Proposals:

Development Proposals: New and untested ideas and technologies or novel customization and application of existing technologies that have the potential to provide benefits outweighing all costs and results that significantly exceed currently deployed solutions. Technologies and products submitted as Development Proposals shall achieve a working prototype or test system.

Field Test Proposals: Products and solutions that have demonstrated significant value in commercial or other production environments but are new to the operating environment within Veterans Affairs. Solutions shall be repeatable and ready for small-scale deployment at the VISN [Veterans Integrated Service Networks] or facility level. Should the results from small-scale deployment prove favorable, the solution shall be scalable to a VA-wide implementation. It is anticipated that an award made in response to this BAA will fund the small-scale field testing.

Identifying Participants

The goal is to have the BAA reach as many suitable companies as possible including a significant number of companies that may be new to Federal contracting. The use of this model, with its staged approach, should encourage participation by entrepreneurs and innovative small businesses.

Developing the BAA

There are two goals for the BAA: (1) Design the BAA to eliminate as many delays and obstacles as possible and automatically mitigate what cannot be eliminated; and (2) Have the proposals responding to the BAA include sufficient information to support comprehensive evaluations and allow the proposal to serve as the Performance Work Statement (PWS) for any resulting contracts. If the resulting proposals are complete, comprehensive, and contain all information necessary to support proposal evaluation and contract award, the acquisition process can be expedited because the contracting officer will not have to hold discussions with the company to resolve areas that are unclear or are contrary to the agency's requirements. If the resulting proposal is sufficiently complete, it can serve as the PWS for any resulting contract, which will also expedite the acquisition process.

The delays and obstacles encountered when awarding a contract for technical work will be specific to each agency, but here are some common issues that can be set forth in the BAA:

1. *IT Governance* – If an agency has IT Governance requirements dictating or forbidding the use of specific hardware or software, this information should be included in the BAA as requirements for all resulting projects. For example, many agencies require the use of the

Windows operating system for client applications and the Linux operating system for back-end server applications. If this is the case, then this information should be a requirement in the BAA. If there are two possible technical options for supporting potential solutions and additional approvals are required for one option but not the other option, consider limiting the company's IT choices for their solution to the option that does not require the additional approvals.

2. *Security* – Different agencies have different security requirements for companies performing work. If there are options or approaches that require fewer approvals than other options or approaches, it may be beneficial to make the option requiring fewer approvals mandatory -- if it will not unduly constrain the resulting prototype development effort. Security requirements and restrictions can always be revisited for successful prototypes when planning for longer term follow-on work.

3. *Intellectual Property and Government Rights* – The BAA needs to clearly state the conditions that will apply to all intellectual property (IP) developed under any contracts resulting from the project and whether the FAR/DFAR (or other agency specific) clauses regarding intellectual property will apply. Additionally, the BAA should state the minimum level of rights the agency is willing to accept, for example, Government Purpose rights, for all work developed under resulting contracts. Companies should also be informed in the BAA that offering to provide the prototype with rights less than the minimum level the agency is willing to accept may negatively impact their proposal evaluation.

4. *Payments* – Although contracts are likely to be firm fixed price, most efforts will involve a series of payments. The BAA should articulate that only offerors invited for full proposals will be asked to provide their desired funding profile, informed by planned expenditures based on calendar quarters. Agencies may alternatively tie each payment into a specific deliverable, for example, invoice #1 corresponds to the delivery of milestone #1. The company can then propose the amount for each scheduled payment. Having all companies follow the same payment schedule and identifying the payment amounts up front eliminates a common time-consuming item for contracting officer discussions with the company and simplifies the management of multiple projects after the award.

5. *Deliverables* – The BAA needs to clearly define what deliverables are associated with any resulting contracts. The deliverables expected depend on the proposal type, but in all cases should provide sufficient information for continual and final evaluation regarding scale-up potential. Such information could come in the form of milestones. For example, the VAi2 BAA required:

Development Proposals shall include milestones that demonstrate achievement of significant design steps, validation of new technologies and/or architectures, completion of work that indicates substantial risk reduction, etc. Prototype delivery and/or demonstration milestones shall be included, if appropriate.

Field Test Proposals shall include milestones that demonstrate significant steps in design, integration, testing, installation, verification, data collection, etc. The proposal shall clearly identify any required interaction with VA resources, data, facilities, etc. Prototype delivery and/or demonstration milestones shall be included, if appropriate.

All Proposals shall clearly identify the risks involved with their proposed solutions, and plans for mitigation of said risks.

6. *Concept Paper Content and Format* — If the BAA provides specific instructions on the content and format of the concept papers and full proposals, it will expedite evaluation of the submissions and make it more likely that companies will include all necessary and relevant information in their submissions. For example, the VAi2 Industry Innovation Competition requested concept papers to include the following content:

   a. Proposed Approach (Technical Summary) – A concise description of the technical approach, describing the architecture, implementation plan, and the impacts and benefits of the proposed innovation. A short statement of the structure and timeline should be included. Clearly outline any technical challenges inherent in the approach and possible solutions for overcoming potential problems.

   b. Supporting Technical Analysis: Address how the proposed technical approach is innovative/revolutionary and how it rises above the current state of practice.

   c. Anticipated Requirements for VA Resources: In addition to the funding requested, please describe any anticipated requirements of VA to make the pilot or field test successful. Examples include software hosting, access to patient data, etc.

  d. Team Expertise: A brief summary of expertise of the key personnel on the project relevant to the program goals. If the team is multi-organizational, a proposed management structure should also be included.

In addition to a cover sheet requesting the Technical Point of Contact's information, the proposal type (Development, Field Test, or both), the cost Rough Order of Magnitude (ROM), and the duration of the proposed work, the VAi2 BAA requested a single-page summary slide containing the following sections: one-line description, one-paragraph summary, key picture/chart, ROM and schedule, and promised impact to the agency. Together, these three documents should support the rapid assessment of the technology landscape while providing enough technical detail to inform full proposal invites. The BAA should also specify page limits for the concept paper—the VAi2 Competition requested papers limited to eight pages in length, including a cover sheet and single-page summary slide.

7. *Full Proposal Content and Format* – When it is time for the second stage of this model, the agency will issue a BAA with specific instructions on the content and format of the full proposal to streamline the evaluation process. For example, the BAA could request to include the following content in the proposal:

  a. Executive Summary – Intended to provide an overview of the salient features of the entire proposal.

  b. Background & Description – A detailed background, discussion and description of the proposed solution, and categorization as a Development Proposal and/or a Field Test Proposal.

  c. Impact – A clear, concise definition of the impact, benefits, and scalability of the solution to the stated area of interest. Additional information such as a description of the current state-of-the-art concerning the proposed technology/approach, a discussion of comparable products, technologies and/or approaches similar to what the company is proposing, and an explanation of why what the company is proposing is of value.

  d. Description of the Solution Design and/or Architecture – Development Proposals should clearly identify the new technology being developed, including a description of the current technology status and the future development to be undertaken. Field Test Proposals should clearly indicate the current level of deployment of the solution and describe the areas where agency deployment involves new or untested usage. The solution description should be written in a clear and concise manner and shall serve as the basis for a PWS should the proposal submission result in a contract award. Any hardware, software, data, or documentation items the company wants to request from the government to support this effort need to be identified in the proposal so potential delays in providing these at the pilot sites can be factored into the proposal evaluation.

e. Feasibility & Methodology – A reasonably complete discussion that details the feasibility and the methodology of the proposed approach(es) and identifies the level of effort to be employed. Risks associated with the proposers' solutions as well as mitigation strategies should be identified and discussed.

f. Unique Capabilities – A presentation of the offeror's unique capabilities and/or specialized experience. The offeror should also identify and provide resumes for key personnel and the principal investigator showing relevant experience.

g. Cost/Price – As a separate volume in the full proposal, the offeror's cost/price proposal should be prepared in a clear and concise manner that accurately reflects the offeror's include all costs expected during the performance of the contract. All details, broken down by cost element, should be prepared for each major task along with supporting rationale. Cost elements include: direct labor, materials, travel, other direct costs, consultants, subcontractors, indirect costs, profit/fee, and desired funding profile. The agency should indicate a preference for Firm Fixed Price (FFP) type contracts.

h. Sub-Contracts or Relevant Collaborations – A description of any proposed sub-contracts or relevant collaborations planned or already in place with industry, government organizations, universities, or other institutions.

i. Past Performance on similar R&D work.

The BAA should specify page limits for the full proposal, split into a technical and cost/price volume. The technical volume should be limited to 50 pages and the cost/price volume should have no limit. This length is sufficient to provide a comprehensive description of the proposals selected from the first round of rapid concept paper evaluations.

Evaluating Proposals and Selecting for Award

The proposal evaluation plan should reserve the right to fund all, some, or none of the concept papers and full proposals received under the BAA solicitation in order to retain the greatest flexibility for the government. The BAA should clearly articulate that an invitation to submit a concept paper or full proposal does *not* guarantee a contract award. The BAA should also specify that all proposals are treated as sensitive competitive information with disclosure, use, or duplication only for purposes of evaluation, and that no funding is available for direct reimbursement of proposal development costs. To support the rapid assessment of innovative technologies, the BAA should emphasize the importance of clear, concise papers and proposals, as below:

> Offerors are advised that the quality of the information presented in the proposal is significantly more important than the quantity. It is desired that the proposals, as briefly as possible, provide details of the technology and the design of the proposed solution, the impact on the stated field of interest, the scalability of the solution, the implementation plan, and the capabilities and expertise/experience of the Offeror as described in the section entitled "Proposal Submission Format."

The evaluation criteria for concept papers and full proposals should be simple, straightforward, and consistent. Six evaluation criteria that work effectively for pilot proposals are:

- The potential impact, benefits, and contributions of the solution to the agency mission areas of interest
- The quality of the proposed solution design
- The quality of the proposed implementation plan
- The scalability of the proposed solution
- The offeror's capabilities, related expertise/experience, past performance, facilities, techniques, or unique combinations of these that are integral factors for the achievement of proposal objectives
- The cost-effectiveness of the solution in proportion to its potential impact/benefits

The evaluation of concept papers and full proposals can be streamlined by requiring that submissions be consist of distinct technical volumes and cost/price volumes. The former requirement orients the technical review committee to appropriate evaluation standards, while the latter better aligns the evaluation criteria to full proposal submissions. To ensure that offerors with strong paper proposals can deliver on them, agencies should thoroughly review financial backgrounds before award decisions are announced. Consistent with the BAA solicitation to offerors, the technical review committee should be clear that the evaluation process is not a competition, even within a topic area. The lack of a common statement of work precludes fair comparisons among offerors.

The technical committee should consist of both subject matter experts and potential agency end users with membership size dictated by the topic area's complexity. For example, the VAi2 2011 Industry Innovation Competition arranged committees of five to fourteen experts depending on topic area. Subject matter experts involved in the identification of topic areas should serve on the technical review committees to more accurately assess if offerors' technologies indeed satisfy agency needs as well as help identify appropriate pilot sites.

Executing the Award

The main objective in executing the awarded contracts is to establish and thoroughly assess pilots of the offerors' technologies such that promising pilots can be rapidly scaled across the agency through follow- on contracts. Additionally, if the company is able to deliver the pilot on schedule and budget and if the pilot has the capabilities and features stipulated in the full proposal, this is a good indication that the company can succeed in subsequent work.

Involving End Users

It is critical for end users to be involved with oversight of the technology aspects of each project, but it is equally important that the technical end users do not have to spend their limited and valuable time on the administrative aspects of the project, especially when most of the projects will not continue into follow-on work and will stop at the end of the contract's period of performance. If many of the issues that could cause delays or obstacles to execution are "designed out" of the program from the beginning, then one person can easily handle the administrative duties for multiple proposals, leaving the technical end users to solely focus on the technical aspects of the work. Offices that have a need for the capabilities potentially offered by the technology and offices that would have to be involved in scaling up the pilot are good sources for technical end users to participate in technical discussions with the company during contract execution.

Managing Risk and Establishing Expectations

Typically working within a 12-24 month period for testing and evaluation, agency pilot sites face several challenges, including unforeseen timing issues, integrating prototype technologies within existing systems, and receiving buy-in from pilot staff. Because the majority of pilot staff may have other, perhaps dominant, work responsibilities, agencies should maximize the number of technical end users, contract organizers, or other interested parties overseeing pilot progress. Unforeseen issues, particularly with larger pilots, may arise from an insufficient number of participants, technological bugs, or not getting participants security clearances in time. To mitigate these challenges, the government's expectations for the company and relevant information on the pilot site should be defined and clearly articulated up front so the company knows what to expect. Very frequent, informal interactions between the company and government personnel should be provided to ensure coordination and adequate progress.

Providing Technical Guidance and Advice

Throughout the solicitation and proposal evaluation process, there should be regular opportunities for the contractors to ask questions of the government agency. Within several weeks of the BAA publication, agencies should host an industry day webinar to provide information for each area of interest and address questions from industry. Informal communication should be encouraged, with all questions and responses posted for all contractors to see to avoid duplication and ensure a fair playing field. Procedural questions could be directed to the agency's technology acquisition center (TAC) and substantive questions to subject matter experts. Questions and responses could be posted on an online forum such as FedBizOpps.gov.

After the announcement of award decisions, communications should be limited solely to offerors participating in pilots. There should also be regular opportunities during the execution of the pilots for the agency's technical end users to ask questions of the company about the work being done, their progress, and their pilot's potential for scaling up. Teleconferences can easily take the place of face-to- face meetings, especially where time or location considerations apply to the personnel participating in these meetings.

The objective is to provide the company with sufficient information about the agency's needs so that the company can develop the most relevant prototype possible given the cost and schedule constraints.

Evaluating Pilots

The monitoring, evaluation, and intervention of technology pilots should be continual, akin to adaptive management—a structured, iterative process of course-correcting that reduces uncertainty over time via system monitoring. Uncertainties associated with introducing a novel technology to a pilot site include its effectiveness, operability, and resistance to adoption. In this way, adaptive management seeks to fulfill short-term objectives while accumulating the knowledge base to optimize long-term pilot outcomes. This process of evaluation and intervention is predicated on frequent and honest dialogue among end users, offerors, and pilot managers.

Once the pilot has been completed, agencies must decide whether the technology is scalable. Such decisions should be informed by the nature of the technology (software vs. hardware), its complexity, and the offerors' financial background and resources. Agencies should also assess the technology landscape to ensure advances have not rendered the pilot technology obsolete, considering the time and cost associated with fully vetting another technology.

Pursuing Follow-on Work

Pilots selected for follow-on work should be transferred to the standard acquisition processes. Technical agency end users who participated in the execution phase of the project are likely candidates for sponsoring the follow-on work. If possible, agencies may cite the pilot as justification for a sole source follow-on contract for the company. Companies with prototypes that are not considered for follow-on work should be notified and provided with constructive feedback as to why their technology was not selected for follow-on work so the company can improve its efforts in the future.

However, the requirements for full and open competition in the Competition in Contracting Act of 1984 may present obstacles for agencies seeking to transition pilots into sole source follow-on contracts. For example, the VAi2 Industry Innovation Competition has observed intense competition for follow-on contracts mandated by full and open competition. In short, agencies must acknowledge and prepare for multiple scenarios in scaling up promising pilot technologies agency-wide.

VAi2 Pilot Successes

Regardless of the outcome of the scale-up phase, agencies can derive significant value from the technology pilots of staged contracts. For example, the VA provided seed funding to VETransfer, a non- profit startup, to create an end-to-end business accelerator for Veteran entrepreneurs, offering individualized mentorship at a physical incubator facility as well as online resources. In its first years since 2011, VETransfer generated 24 startups, raised nearly $1.4 million, created 89 jobs, and is scaling nationwide. Moreover, around 400 Veterans have completed the three-month online programs.

Another awardee, Agilex Technologies, developed a system that enables providers to access electronic health record information on mobile devices. Most pilot participants (55-70%) reported a positive impact on their productivity and ability to communicate with patients and other providers. The pilot also demonstrated the feasibility of deploying mobile devices in a clinical setting on VA networks.

A final example is MedRed's TBI Toolbox, which enables care providers to continuously develop, share, and administer the latest treatment methods in the rapidly evolving field of polytrauma care. Pilot users project the TBI Toolbox will eliminate collection of over 19,000 paper forms per year if deployed across the VA enterprise. When asked for their feedback, 74% of end users strongly agreed or agreed the system provides process improvement; 68% of users strongly agreed or agreed the system improves continuity of care; and 84% of users are extremely satisfied or very satisfied with system scoring and reporting.

Conclusion

The staged acquisitions described above are effective at rapidly funneling many private sector technologies to both identify and validate options for meeting an agency's particular requirements. This approach, which uses the BAA acquisition method, can be easily tailored and customized to meet the specific requirements and constraints of different government agencies. Among the innovative contracting models, staged contracts can uniquely:

- Harness the ingenuity of the American people to provide government solutions through less burdensome concept papers

- Effectively utilize limited government resources to rapidly assess many technologies and make results-based decisions regarding further investment
- Facilitate knowledge transfer from the government to small businesses, especially during pilots, to better enable the small businesses to support the government's requirements
- Ensure extensive agency end user involvement, buy-in, and subsequent technology adoption

MILESTONE-BASED COMPETITIONS: MAXIMIZING VALUE FROM SMALL BUSINESSES

Overview

Government agencies need the ability to attract innovative approaches to well-documented problems, while minimizing cost, risk, and liability. Milestone-based contracts allow government agencies to accomplish these goals by financing the completion of authorized work, in the form of milestones, withholding payment until the agreed-upon milestone is completed. In crafting the solicitation, the government establishes a series of milestones, each with well-defined requirements, a deadline, and an assigned monetary value. *Competitive* milestone-based contracts further the concept by promoting competition among a stable pool of selected contractors through a series of clear, technically feasible milestones. By forgoing a bulky, long-term deliverable in favor of a series of achievable milestones, these contracts encourage participation from traditionally underrepresented contractors, such as small businesses and high-growth startups. As outlined in the following section, competitive milestone-based contracts also provide agencies considerable flexibility in contract financing and solicitation.

In general, competitive milestone-based contracts work as follows:

1. *Announce:* agencies release a broad solicitation for contractors to compete through a series of milestones, each with a defined problem statement and monetary value.
2. *Select:* agencies select a pool of competing contractors following the initial solicitation.

3. *Launch:* agencies announce which milestones are under competition and provide more specific language on technical constraints and deadlines.

4. *Maintain:* agencies award first milestone winners and decide when to place the remaining milestones under competition, depending on fiscal constraints. The government is not compelled to compete any milestones beyond the first, and no contractor is entitled to award money beyond the minimum.

Embrace Flexibility

Contracting flexibility is imperative for resource-constrained government agencies to attract innovation from small businesses. Competitive milestone-based contracts, by forgoing a bulky, long-term deliverable in favor of a series of achievable milestones, encourage participation from traditionally underrepresented contractors, such as small businesses and high-growth startups. The unique combination of attributes in these contracts—firm-fixed price, indefinite delivery/indefinite quantity (IDIQ), and performance incentives—maximizes value delivered to government and places full financial responsibility on the contractors. The simplicity, transparency, and clear, technically feasible series of requirements surrounding competitive milestone-based contracts encourage the participation of small businesses. This paper outlines some of the considerations in establishing such a program, based on the NASA ILDD project.

Flexible in Funding

Government agencies may find significant flexibility in financing competitive milestone-based contracts. Beyond the established minimum deliverable and payment, agencies may choose which milestones to put in play and withhold others depending on available funds. Moreover, the firm-fixed price of each milestone shifts the risk to the contractors, providing agencies expected or better-than-expected overall program costs. As each milestone is independent of another, agencies have no ongoing liabilities following the conclusion of one milestone, and possess the flexibility to modify or freeze the contract. Competitive milestone-based contracts may also be more cost-effective than traditional contracts. For example, the NASA ILDD contracts, under their first milestone "Critical Component Demonstration," paid only $500,000 rather than the typical $3-5 million for propulsion data from innovative rocket injectors using green propellants. Additional flexibility is conferred to agencies through their ability to establish minimum and maximum accumulated award amounts for each contractor.

Flexible in Solicitation

Competitive milestone-based contracts also offer government agencies additional flexibility in the crafting of solicitations. Specifically, the public call for proposals—using a BAA—need only contain the statement of objectives, baseline requirements, and property/data rights; the details of individual milestones can be augmented with greater specificity later, once the contractor pool is established. The same applies to future milestones not currently underway. This provides government agencies the flexibility to introduce or modify downstream milestone requirements should needs change. The initial solicitation encourages small business participation with its simplicity— instead of the typical hundred or more pages, the NASA ILDD BAA spanned only 18 pages including appendices. The solicitation's open- ended nature, without government micro-managing solutions, emphasized contractor creativity. However, these same qualities require agencies to have an effective procurement office to assist applicants and ensure adequate government engagement. In short, competitive milestone-based contracts offer agencies a relatively cost-effective, simple, and adaptable mechanism to attract small business innovation.

Challenges & Limitations

Flexibility in both funding and solicitation result in unique agency challenges. Government agencies must remain cognizant of contractors' different development schedules in announcing new, active milestones to maximize competition. Another challenge arises in the delicate balancing of the initial solicitation's open-ended requirements to foster innovation and providing sufficient information to contractors. This balancing may be an iterative process where agencies publicly post clarifying responses to questions. Contractors may also misrepresent their relationship with the government agency for financial benefit; agencies may consider including language regulating such behavior. After the contract concludes, contractors, especially small businesses, may seek funding from foreign sponsors; agencies should expect such situations.

There are limitations to the applicability of competitive milestone-based contracts. These contracts may not be suitable for the development of complex, incremental systems, such as the engineering of an entire space shuttle. As milestones may rely on previous milestones' solutions, scenarios of technological incompatibility across contractors or intellectual property rights thickets may arise. Moreover, if the government agency's mission includes the public dissemination of knowledge, it may become frustrated by the lack of insight into contractors' operations and progress. Finally, well-defined milestone requirements may preclude agencies from expanding their scope, though new milestones can be introduced.

Using This Innovative Model

The main objective is to design the competitive milestone-based contract solicitation to result in a large number of good proposals describing innovative technologies, ideas, and approaches relevant to the agency's requirements. A second, but equally important, objective is to design the RFP so it expedites the overall process by clarifying any areas or issues that could cause delays in understanding specific milestone requirements. The BAA mechanism can serve as the basis of the acquisition effort.

Identifying the Problems/Requirements

The problems included in the BAA need to be thought of as "bait" to attract and challenge companies to focus on solutions for these problems. In the initial solicitation to select the pool of contractors, requirements can be high level, allowing applicants to pursue innovative yet technically sound approaches. The key to the problems is to provide enough background information so a company can make an intelligent assessment about what would be required and desired in a solution. Additionally, even if a company decides to not submit a proposal, the background information provided about the problems/requirements can start to educate industry on the agency's requirements, which assists companies to submit relevant proposals in the future. Milestone requirements, however, must be very specific with a defined result, especially after selection of the competing pool of contractors. For example, a NASA ILDD contract milestone in the initial solicitation follows:

"CLIN 1: Critical Component Demonstration

NASA's objective is to acquire data as a result of conducting a critical component demonstration test of an item that was one of the top 10 risks as identified in the participant's SDR data package. The participant will be asked to provide information similar to the following:

a. *The component should be classified as flight-like with respect to form, fit and function.*

b. *The functional performance parameters should be defined with allowable margins. For example, 'the temperature sensor shall provide measurement data in the range of -100 deg C up to +100 C with an error of no more than +/- 1 deg C'.*

c. *The component should be tested in an Earth standard laboratory environment. This should be a space-qualification test (full-up) under operational environment conditions (temperature, pressure, vibration, etc.).*

d. *The component should meet the identified functional performance parameters."*

The expectations for problems/requirements should focus on what can realistically be achieved in the allowed timeframe. If specific requirements or constraints exist for a particular problem and its potential solutions, this information should also be included in the problem description. Some common specific constraints are: minimum performance requirements, the use of certain software or platforms, minimum data amounts, the use of a particular set of test data, etc. Another type of information very useful to companies when crafting their response is a description of approaches or technologies that the agency is not interested in. The "Not Interested In" list could be common approaches which have been tried so often that there is very little value in trying it again. It could also be approaches the agency knows will not work effectively based on internal research. The reasons the agency is not interested do not have to be included with the description of the "Not Interested In" approach/technology.

With a clear articulation of the problems to be addressed, contracts can encourage significant private investment tied to government-established milestones. For example, several NASA ILDD contractors had private investments dependent on the successful completion of NASA milestones, amplifying the incentives to deliver maximum value to government, strengthening the contractors, and recruiting de facto private partners. Moreover, the six teams participating in the NASA ILDD program were all participating in the Google Lunar X PRIZE, which offers a total of $30 million in prizes.

Engaging the Future End Users

Potential end users should be engaged as early as possible, and the end users should be the main participants in identifying the problems/requirements. End users should be identified from among the subject matter experts and power users in an office because they are most likely to truly understand where the gaps exist in their technologies and what new capabilities are needed to take their work to the next level. When an office contributes some of its own funding to support the acquisition effort, the office is much more likely to support continued engagement by the end users.

Relating milestone requirements to how end users will use the deliverables towards the agency's larger mission provides contractors valuable context. For example, the NASA ILDD BAA articulated the purpose of purchasing technical data arising from commercial development of small, robotic lunar landers:

> "The ILDD procurement will allow NASA's Lunar Lander Project Office to increase its knowledge and understanding of the design, testing, and flight lessons to be learned through the use of these landers. Additionally, this information will enable the Lunar Lander Project Office to quickly and efficiently implement a plan for building and testing relevant components of lander hardware to be utilized in future human and robotic landers. Lunar mission scenarios producing data of interest to NASA may include performing lunar landing using a human mission profile, identification of hazards during landing, precision landing, and extended duration operations."

Constraining the Solution Space

While it is important to not constrain the ideas, it is very important to constrain the support technologies used to implement the deliverable to give each technology its best chance of being integrated into existing systems if the technology proves successful. Unlike the private sector, the reality of many government systems is they are not going to undergo any large scale replacement and, instead, need to evolve in place to incorporate new technologies and capabilities. This makes it necessary to constrain the solution space so potential new capabilities are designed to facilitate integration with existing systems. For example, if most existing systems at an agency use Linux servers and Windows clients, then this type of architecture should be a requirement for potential new capabilities. If the potential capability does not have the flexibility to use the specified architecture, it likely will not be able to be used regardless of its potential benefit. Thus, it is best to discover this issue early. Some good constraints to consider are:

- A preference for using Open Source software where suitable software is available to minimize licensing costs
- No reliance or dependency on proprietary data formats or data storage mechanisms
- Web-enabled GUIs and user facing applications
- Software developed using a common language such as C, C++, or Java
- Use of specific standards or protocols

Solutions based on commercial products are generally less successful than solutions based on open technologies because commercial products may be less cutting-edge and innovative due to the amount of time it takes to bring a commercial product to market. Additionally, commercial products generally are associated with significant licensing fees that can be unrealistic for widespread government usage.

Identifying Participants
The goal is to have the BAA reach as many suitable companies as possible including a significant number of companies that may be new to Federal contracting. The use of this model, with its shortened timeframe of producing a prototype in 6 months or less, and at a dollar value under the simplified acquisition threshold, should encourage participation by entrepreneurs and innovative small businesses. However, recognize that if the agency decides to go into production of the prototype, some of the companies may lack adequate cash flow management or have difficulties adjusting to the government's sometimes lengthy payment schedule, complex Federal Acquisition Regulation (FAR) and Defense Federal Acquisition Regulation (DFAR) contract clauses, and lengthy government acquisition cycles. Therefore, it may be beneficial to prescreen companies for interest using a market survey or some other advance notice of the upcoming acquisition to ensure they understand the requirements of a Federal acquisition.

Developing the BAA

There are two goals for the BAA: (1) Design the BAA to eliminate as many delays and obstacles as possible and automatically mitigate what cannot be eliminated; and (2) Have the proposals responding to the BAA include sufficient information to support comprehensive evaluations. Competitive milestone- based contract BAAs need only contain the statement of objectives, baseline milestone requirements, and intellectual property and government rights; the details of individual milestones can be augmented with greater specificity later, once the contractor pool is established. If the resulting proposals are complete, comprehensive, and contain all information necessary to support proposal evaluation and contract award, the acquisition process can be expedited because the Contracting Officer will not have to hold discussions with the company to resolve areas that are unclear or are contrary to the Government's requirements.

The delays and obstacles encountered when awarding a contract for technical work will be specific to each agency but here are some common issues that can be designed out of the BAA:

1. *IT Governance* – If an agency has IT Governance requirements dictating or forbidding the use of specific hardware or software, this information should be included in the BAA as requirements for all resulting projects. For example, many agencies standardized on the use of the Windows operating system for client applications and on the use of the Linux operating system for back end server applications. If this is the case, then this information should be a requirement in the BAA. If there are two possible technical options for supporting potential solutions and additional approvals are required for one option but not the other option, consider limiting the company's IT choices for their deliverable to the option that does not require the additional approvals.

2. *Intellectual Property and Government Rights* – The BAA needs to clearly state the conditions that will apply to all Intellectual Property developed under any contracts resulting from the project and whether the FAR/DFAR (or other agency specific) clauses regarding intellectual property will apply. Additionally, the BAA should state the minimum level of rights the agency is willing to accept, for example, Government Purpose rights, for all work developed under resulting contracts. Companies should also be informed in the BAA

that offering to provide property rights less than the minimum level the agency is willing to accept may negatively impact their proposal evaluation.

3. *Payments* – The BAA should clearly establish the total value of the contracts, the maximum award to any one offeror, and the minimum order. For example, the NASA ILDD BAA established $30.1 million as the total value, with a maximum of $10 million award to any one offeror. Additionally, the BAA mandated all offerors submit a written System Definition Review (SDR) data package within 21 days of contract award, which would satisfy the $10,000 minimum order, and before competition for milestones. The SDR provided vital information on the selected offeror's proposed system architecture/ design and the flowdown to all functional elements of the system. Beyond this SDR, offerors selected to be in the IDIQ pool were not obligated to compete/bid on every milestone and were not guaranteed to receive any additional task orders or payments as agencies may choose which milestones to put in play and withhold others depending on the financing available.

4. *Deliverables* – The BAA needs to clearly define what deliverables are associated with the minimum order and the milestones. If there are requirements for a deliverable that are beyond what is described in the Contract Line Item Numbers (CLINs) for that deliverable, these additional requirements need to be clearly noted in the BAA. The BAA should specify that each CLIN will be competed in an IDIQ fashion with the government evaluating proposals based on criteria specified in the associated request for a task plan. The BAA should also specify the deadline and submission requirements for the minimum order.

5. *Proposal Content and Format*– If the BAA provides specific instructions on the content and format of the proposals, it will expedite evaluation of the proposals and make it more likely that companies will include all necessary and relevant information in their proposals. For example, the BAA could request the proposal to include the following content:

    a. Executive Summary – Intended to provide an overview of the salient features of the entire proposal.

    b. Technical Approach – A description of the offeror's technical approach with sufficient detail for the government agency to evaluate its reasonableness and innovativeness, as well as the offeror's performance on previous, relevant projects. For example, the NASA ILDD BAA requested the technical documents: Concept of Operations, Conceptual Vehicle Design, and Demonstrated Performance with Relevant Technical Endeavors. Respectively, these documents described the general description of the proposed lunar mission, major components of the proposed vehicle, and performance on past endeavors and their relation to the BAA. These requirements were relatively open-ended, purposefully crafted to elicit innovative approaches.

c. Business Model — A description of the offeror's business strategy for successful completion of the proposed technical approach. Important information includes: the company's relevant experience, availability of adequate financial resources and financial commitments, access to technical equipment and facilities, and team members with relevant experience along with organizational structure. The business model should also require a financial plan, describing the funding available by government fiscal year that will enable the successful completion of the proposed technical approach as well as potential threats to the plan.

d. Value Proposal — A description of the intellectual property rights the offerors propose to confer beyond internal government use, and a complementary written justification that the government is receiving products of value commensurate with the financial award of each milestone.

e. Sub-Contracts or Relevant Collaborations – A description of any proposed sub-contracts or relevant collaborations planned or already in place with industry, government organizations, universities, or other institutions. Collaborations with foreign entities must be clearly identified so the government agency can arrange with sponsoring foreign agencies for the proposed participation on a no-exchange-of-funds basis.

f. Other Parties – Identification of other parties to whom the proposal has been or will be sent, in compliance with U.S. export control laws and regulations.

g. Deliverables – A detailed description of all deliverables to be provided to the government as a result of the work and in accordance with the requirements in the Contract Data Requirements List.

h. Past Performance in similar R&D work.

The BAA should also specify page limits for the Technical and Management proposals. For milestone- based contracts, a 10 page Technical Approach; 10 page Business Model, with business strategy and financial plan; and 5 page value proposal should be sufficient. This length is sufficient to provide a comprehensive description of the work and it can still support relatively rapid proposal evaluations.

Evaluating Proposals and Selecting for Award

The proposal evaluation plan should reserve the right to fund all, some, or none of the proposals received under the BAA solicitation in order to retain the greatest flexibility for the government. The plan should also specify that all proposals are treated as sensitive competitive information with disclosure only for purposes of evaluation, and that no funding is available for direct reimbursement of proposal development costs. The proposal evaluation criteria should be simple and straightforward. Three evaluation criteria that work effectively for milestone-based contracts are:

1. Technical Approach
   a. Scientific and technical merit
   b. Innovativeness and reasonableness
   c. Viability and practicality of technical approach
   d. Previously demonstrated performance
2. Business Merit
   a. Realistic and reasonable business strategy
   b. Funding profile, with identified threats and mitigation
   c. Applicability and validity to proposal
3. Value Merit
   a. Government property/data rights
   b. Risk Management
   c. Cost Realism

A two phase evaluation process works well for milestone-based contracts. If many proposals are received or if different proposals require different technical expertise, then different reviewers could be assigned to each proposal so the same three people do not have to evaluate each proposal. In phase 1 for each proposal, an assembled peer review team could assign a rating to each evaluation criteria using confidence level ratings: high, medium, and low confidence. High confidence proposals are of exceptional merit in the specific evaluation factor, are likely to satisfy requirements identified in the solicitation, and any unfavorable observations are minor. Medium confidence proposals are of appreciable merit, provide a reasonable likelihood of satisfying requirements, and unfavorable observations moderately detract from the proposal. Low confidence proposals fail to demonstrate appreciable merit, are not likely to satisfy requirements, and unfavorable observations are significant.

Confidence ratings assigned to each proposal's evaluation criteria can then be aggregated into an overall rating for the proposal. Each proposal could receive one of three category ratings: category I, II, or III. Category I proposals are recommended for acceptance; they are well-conceived, offer scientific innovation and sound strategy, supported by responsible contractors and sufficient resources, and confer desired property/data rights. Category II proposals are recommended for acceptance, but at a lower priority than Category I proposals; they are scientifically innovative, supported by a responsible contractor and adequate resources, confer acceptable property/data rights, but require further development technically. Category III proposals are not recommended for acceptance; they are not technically sound or do not meet agency needs.

In phase 2, a technical peer review is conducted by a small group of stakeholders to consider the evaluation information provided by the previous peer review team and to determine which of the specific proposals recommended for acceptance into the competitive milestone-based contract represent the best value to the government.

Executing the Award

The main objective of milestone-based contracts is to encourage innovation satisfying government requirements at much lower government cost, risk, and liability. As contractors are incentivized to produce maximum value for agencies under strict timelines, agencies avoid intensive, hands-on work throughout. Moreover, milestone-based contracts' flexibility in financing and requirements allows agencies to adapt milestones while executing the program. Contractors that fail to meet milestone requirements incur minimal, defined agency costs, allowing agencies to only reward success. However, the success of milestone-based contracts still depends on agency coordination of contractors and deliverables transfer, management of remaining risk, and provision of technical guidance. Promising contractors may be selected for follow-on work under standard acquisition processes or other innovative contracting approaches.

Involving End Users

Government agencies participating in milestone-based payment systems will find their greatest challenges in coordinating contractors, especially with the limited insight into their progress. In order to ensure the maximum level of competition among contractors for each task request, agencies must be cognizant of each contractor's development schedule and find a juncture in time attractive to most contractors for announcing new requests. Competition can be further fostered through informal communications and technical guidance. Another unique problem may arise when contractors misrepresent their relationship with the government agency as advertisement for their goods or services. Agencies should clearly outline policies regulating such practices to curb public misunderstanding of milestone-based payment's hands-off nature as a formal endorsement. While milestone-based contracts provide agencies financial flexibility through sequestration, agencies should establish and communicate expectations on which milestones have secured funding and which have not. Finally, agencies should coordinate with contractors should new requirements be introduced to downstream milestones.

Managing Risk and Establishing Expectations

The key to effectively managing milestone-based projects is to allow the company to manage all execution risk and avoid any dependencies on the government for information, approvals, or other items. Though not as detailed in the initial BAA, task requests for further milestones should clearly articulate the government's expectations so the company knows what to expect in terms of progress checkpoints, deliverable requirements (e.g., prototype demonstrations), and amount of technical guidance and advice that will be provided. Frequent interactions between the company and government personnel such as participation of government personnel in the company's daily technical meetings should be avoided to minimize adding too much government bias to the effort and avoid shifting additional risk onto the government.

Providing Technical Guidance and Advice

Because of the open-ended nature of the initial BAA, there should be regular opportunities throughout the execution of milestones for the contractors to ask questions of the government agency. To address these questions and gain insight into the contractors' progress, agencies could establish mini-milestones or progress checkpoints, with no additional funding involved. Informal communication should be encouraged, with all questions and responses posted for all contractors to see to avoid duplication and ensure a fair playing field. Teleconferences can easily take the place of face-to-face meetings, especially when time or location considerations apply to the personnel participating in these meetings. The objective is to provide the company with sufficient information about the government's needs that the company can be comfortable in its understanding of the deliverable's nature and scope.

Coordinating Award & Deliverable Hand-off

Comprehensive vetting of the deliverable should occur prior to selection and award for each milestone. There will be variation in vetting and hand-off depending on each milestone's requirements (e.g., data formatting) and deliverable (e.g., prototype, data, etc.). Prototypes should be subjected to a demonstration to provide an effective assessment of the work that has been done and should clearly illustrate how the technology could potentially be applied to mission requirements. The demonstration should be held under pseudo-operational conditions as determined by the technical end users. Data collected should be evaluated to comply with all specified requirements. Government agencies should not hesitate in asking clarifying questions based on observed results, even if the results comply with requirements or threaten to reasonably postpone the delivery date. If questions are asked post-award, responses to these questions should not affect the rating of the contractor's overall performance for future milestones. These clarifications inform government use of the deliverable and promote future communication.

Pursuing Follow-on Work

Given the milestone-based contract's rewarding of defined, stand-alone deliverables, follow-on work is not expected. However, if additional, related work is sought, the agency should evaluate the proposed deliverable's risk and complexity. As detailed earlier, if the follow-on work involves complex or incremental systems unsuitable for milestone-based contracts, agencies should consider standard acquisition processes or other innovative contracting approaches, such as incentive prizes.

Under standard acquisition processes, end users of the deliverable within the agency—and in other agencies or private firms (with rights from the contractor)—are likely candidates for sponsoring the follow-on work. Solicitations for follow-on work could involve only the current pool of milestone-based payment contractors, a subset of the pool, the public, or a set of prescreened companies. Given milestone-based contracting's attractiveness to small businesses, agencies should expect and consider situations where supported businesses later seek foreign funding.

Milestone Based Competition Successes

The NASA Innovative Lunar Demonstrations Data (ILDD) program illustrates the promise of competitive milestone-based contracts. The NASA ILDD program intends to purchase specific data related to lunar exploration resulting from commercial development of small, robotic lunar landers. The program attracted underrepresented organizations, including small businesses, non-profits, new startups, and university consortia before ultimately selecting six teams. All six teams are participating in the Google Lunar X PRIZE, which provides a total of $30 million in prizes to privately funded teams to safely land a robot on the moon's surface, have the robot traverse 500 meters, and send data back to Earth. Moreover, the six teams participating in the NASA ILDD program were not established contractors; though most had identified private investors and crafted a business case, none had ever contracted with the government.

The NASA ILDD program awards small, firm-fixed price, indefinite delivery/indefinite quantity (IDIQ) contracts over the course of five years, with a total value of as much as $30.1 million. Multiple awards are possible, with a minimum data purchase of $10,000 for each selected contractor. Individual awardees can earn as much as $10.1 million.

Conclusion

The acquisition approach described in this section can be very effective at attracting innovative solutions from small businesses to address well-documented problems, while minimizing government cost, risk, and liability. This approach, which uses the BAA acquisition method, can easily be tailored and customized to meet the specific requirements and constraints of different government agencies. Among the innovative contracting models, competitive milestone-based contracts can uniquely:

- Strengthen small businesses through more accessible financing and recruitment of private investment
- Maximize value and innovation delivered to government on specific, concrete agency challenges
- Ensure government flexibility in financing and solicitation given limited resources

INCENTIVE PRIZES: SOURCING SOLUTIONS FROM CITIZEN SOLVERS

Overview

Over the past three years, the Obama Administration has taken important steps to make incentive prizes a standard tool for open innovation in every Federal agency's toolbox. In his September 2009 *Strategy for American Innovation*, President Obama called on all agencies to increase their use of prizes and challenges to address some of our Nation's most pressing challenges. In March 2010, the Office of Management and Budget (OMB) issued a policy framework[4] to guide agencies in using prizes to mobilize American ingenuity and advance their respective core missions. In September 2010, the Administration launched Challenge.gov[5], a one-stop shop where entrepreneurs and citizen solvers can find public-sector prize competitions. To date, that site has featured more than 300 prize offerings from over 50 agencies. The use of prizes in the public sector has expanded under the America COMPETES Reauthorization Act of 2010[6], which granted all Federal agencies authority to conduct prize competitions to spur innovation, solve tough problems, and advance their missions.

Benefits of Prizes in the Public Sector

Prize administrators in the public sector are reaping the rewards of well-designed incentive prizes. Specifically, prizes enable the Federal government to:

- **Pay only for success and establish an ambitious goal without having to predict which team or approach is most likely to succeed.** Contracts and grants are awarded based on proposals for future work, forcing agencies to value past performance at the expense of disruptive innovation. With a focus on proven results, prizes empower untapped talent to deliver unexpected solutions to tough problems.

- **Reach beyond the "usual suspects" to increase the number of minds tackling a problem.** Prizes are one tool to tap the top talent and best ideas wherever they lie, sourcing breakthroughs from a broad pool of both known and unknown sources of innovation in a given industry.

- **Bring out-of-discipline perspectives to bear.** Empirical research[7] conducted by Harvard Business School finds that breakthrough solutions are most likely to come from outside the scientific discipline or at the intersection of two fields of study.

- **Increase cost-effectiveness to maximize the return on taxpayer dollars.** As teams compete not just for the cash purse, but also for the associated validation, prestige, and satisfaction that results from solving important problems, prizes incent significant additional investment, leveraging the prize purse's impact.

- **Inspire risk-taking by offering a level playing field through credible rules and robust judging mechanisms.** Prizes give entrepreneurs and innovators license to pursue an endorsed stretch goal that otherwise would have been considered overly audacious. Clear target metrics and validation protocols defined for the judging of a prize can themselves become defining tools for the subject industry or field.

Prize Types and Potential Outcomes

Experts often make a distinction between "recognition" prizes that honor past achievements and "inducement" or "incentive" prizes that encourage participants in the competition to achieve a particular goal. In a 2009 report[8], McKinsey identified six prize archetypes that provide a useful framework for identifying types of prizes that can best achieve different types of goals:

- **Exemplar Prizes** that define excellence within an area.
- **Point Solution Prizes** that aim to spur development of solutions for a particular well-defined problem. Solutions can include software applications, algorithms, predictive models, ideas, business plans, policy proposals, designs, or prototypes.
- **Market Stimulation Prizes** that try to establish the viability of a market to address a potential market failure, mobilize additional

human talent and financial capital to jumpstart the development of a new industry, or change public perceptions about what is possible.

- **Exposition Prizes** that are designed to highlight a broad range of promising ideas practices, attract attention, and mobilize capital to further develop the winning innovations.
- **Participation Prizes** that create value during and after the competition − not through conferral of the prize award itself but through their role in encouraging contestants to change their behavior or develop new skills that may have beneficial effects during and beyond the competition.
- **Network Prizes** that build networks and strengthen communities by organizing winners into new problem-solving communities that can deliver more impact than individual efforts.

A 2014 Deloitte University Press report, *The Craft of Prize Design − Lessons from the Public Sector*,[9] reviewed over 400 public-sector prizes and noted that prize designers − rather than selecting a particular prize type − are increasingly customizing prize design to target specific desired outcomes along two dimensions:

- Developing ideas, technologies, products, or services
  - Attract new ideas
  - Build prototypes and launch pilots
  - Stimulate markets
- Engaging people, organizations, and communities
  - Raise awareness
  - Mobilize action
  - Inspire transformation

Most prizes target outcomes along both dimensions − prize designers should apply the elements of prize design with desired outcomes in mind.

Incentive prizes are one type of "pull mechanism" − results-based market incentives designed to overcome market failures and catalyze innovation. Other pull mechanisms include:

- **Advance Market Commitments**: Binding commitments to purchase, or to subsidize purchase, of a certain volume of a product at a fixed prize, if the product meets pre-defined performance characteristics.

One example is the GAVI Alliance advance market commitment for pneumococcal vaccine.[10]

- Similarly, an Advance Purchase Guarantee guarantees payment in the event that a buyer fails to honor a commitment to purchase.

- *Non*-binding commitments to purchase products can provide market pull, if there is both a clearly defined performance specification and a strong expression of interest from potential buyers. For example, in June 2013, the Department of Energy put together a coalition of the Federal government and over 200 major commercial building partners that issued a challenge to U.S. manufacturers: "If you can build wireless sub- meters that cost less than $100 apiece and enable us to identify opportunities to save money by saving energy, we will buy them."[11] In 2011, the Department of Energy put together a similar and successful challenge for energy-efficient and cost-effective commercial air conditioners, with the first manufacturer meeting the challenge in May 2012.[12]

- **Buyer's Consortia**: Cooperative agreements between purchasers of products that leverage the combined buying power of those purchasers to drive down the price of products, such as a buyer's consortium set up for Maine school districts to purchase specialized software and specific assistive technology devices.[13]

- **Pay-for-Success Bonds**: Under a Pay for Success bond[14], also known as a social impact bond, the financing organization and the Federal, state or local government enter into a contract that specifies the population to be served, the outcomes to be achieved, the measurement methodology to be used, and the schedule of payments to be made. The financing organization works with philanthropic and other investors to invest in innovative, data-driven service providers that can achieve results. One example of a pay-for-success bond program is an initiative in New York targeted at reducing recidivism in adult males, supported by Goldman Sachs, Bloomberg Philanthropies, and MRDC.[15]

- **Milestone-based Payments**: Payment terms in a standard grant or contract in which the payment for each performance milestone established in the statement of work is not made until the milestone is proven to have been achieved. One example of this approach has been successfully demonstrated in NASA's Commercial Orbital Transportation Services (COTS) program.[16]

- **Priority Review Vouchers**: An accelerated regulatory review offered to products that meet certain performance or cost criteria, such as the FDA Innovation Pathway[17] and USPTO's Patents for Humanity.[18]
- **Patent Buyout**: An offer to buy out the patent rights to a product that meets specified performance conditions at a set price (price for patent usually marked up over market value; followed by placing of the patent into the public domain to encourage competition for commercialization of the product). One example is the purchase of the patent for the Daguerreotype process by the French government in 1839.[19]

Trends in Incentive Prizes

As incentive prizes increase in use in the private and public sectors, new trends are emerging. For example, while many well-known incentive prizes are focused on catalyzing technology R&D, prize administrators are increasingly using incentive prizes to drive behavior change, market adoption of existing solutions and interventions, and progress in areas of social policy such as health, energy use, economic development, and education.

In addition, public-sector prize administrators are increasingly partnerships to increase effectiveness and leverage during prize design and administration. [20]

As more incentive prizes and pull mechanism initiatives are being designed and launched, a growing community of prize designers, administrators, sponsors, and vendors has formed to share best practices and lessons learned. For example, the General Services Administration (GSA) manages a listserv and training events for more than 500 Federal prize administrators.[21] In addition, training events are held for Federal prize administrators, as well as philanthropic and private-sector partners, such as an event in June 2012 hosted by the White House Office of Science and Technology Policy, the Case Foundation, and the Joyce Foundation.[22]

Using This Innovative Model

In December 2010, Congress passed the America COMPETES Reauthorization Act, providing all Federal agencies broad authority to conduct prize competitions as called for by the President. Under the Act, agencies have authority to establish ambitious prizes to advance national priorities:

- **Scope**: The Act authorizes agencies to conduct any prize competition that will "stimulate innovation that has the potential to advance the mission of the respective agency."
- **Size**: Agencies can offer up to a $50 million prize without further consultation with Congress.
- **Multi-Sector Partnerships**: The Act allows agencies to solicit and accept philanthropic and private sector funds to support a prize purse or the competition's design and administration.

For more information on the prize authority in the America COMPETES Reauthorization Act, please see the Fact Sheet and Frequently Asked Questions memorandum[23] developed jointly by policy and legal staff in the Office of Science and Technology Policy and OMB.

As discussed in OMB's March 2010 memorandum[24], agencies can consider conducting prizes under other authorities such as agency-specific authorities (such as those that apply to DOD, DOE, and NASA); procurement authority such as that provided by the Federal Acquisition Regulation (FAR); authority to award grants, participate in cooperative agreements, or both; and authority related to "necessary expense" doctrine, among others.

Agencies, including the Department of Health and Human Services (HHS)[25] and the Environmental Protection Agency (EPA) are establishing strategies and policies to expand their use of the new prize authority. The General Service Administration launched a new contract vehicle (Schedule 541 4G)[26] to decrease the amount of time required for agencies to tap the private-sector expertise that is so critical to early success. A virtual Center of Excellence for Collaborative Innovation[27], led by NASA, is providing guidance to agencies on the full lifecycle of prizes, from design through implementation to post-prize evaluation.

Identifying the Problems/Requirements

Assess gaps and opportunities. The first step in designing a successful incentive prize is to engage in problem definition to identify a problem or opportunity that meaningfully impacts program goals, mission, and strategy and that can feasibly be addressed in part or in whole through an incentive prize. Consider:

- What are critical program milestones, and where are there gaps in reaching those milestones?

- Is it unclear who to turn to when creating a solution? Would tapping into new solvers or a very broad pool of solvers be beneficial?
- Where are new thinking and new ideas needed?
- Can the objective reasonably be achieved in a feasible time frame given current trends in science, technology, and social policy?
- Are there financial or non-monetary incentives (under your organization's control or under the control of potential partner organizations) that could motivate solvers to focus on the problem or opportunity?

Draft Challenge Statement. Draft a statement that describes the problem, gap, or opportunity, as well as the relevant scientific, technological, or social trends that make it likely that the challenge can be addressed.

Deconstruct the problem. Can it be broken into more specific milestones or targets? These component milestones could each be the basis of an incentive prize, or they could represent phases of one multi- stage competition.

Engaging the Future End Users

Get stakeholder input. For complex issues, consider enlisting assistance with selecting a prize type and designing the target criteria and rules. Consult a diverse set of experts and stakeholders through targeted interviews. Note that the America COMPETES prize authority encourages agencies to consult widely within and outside the Federal government when selecting topics for prize competitions and throughout the lifecycle of a prize. One way to enlist input and ideas in prize design is to host one or more workshops to provide an opportunity for brainstorming and building out prize concepts. Agencies may also empanel advisory committees. Some prize administration vendors, including several on GSA Schedule 541 4G, provide services to assist Federal agencies with designing prizes through expert consultations and facilitated workshops.

Identify Federal resources. A key step in prize design is to identify resources that could be made available to entrants in the competition that would improve or strengthen submissions. For example, a number of Federal agencies have made government data and data standards available to developers to improve entries in apps competitions such as Apps for Energy. And in the Progressive Insurance Automotive X PRIZE, semi-finalist teams were given vouchers for consulting services from private consulting firms and national laboratories in order to allow competing teams to improve their designs. Federal resources can also assist with competition judging and validation of winning solutions. For example, in the Wendy Schmidt Oil Cleanup X Challenge, a Department of Interior testing facility was used to host physical and laboratory testing of finalist prototype designs for high-performing oil cleanup equipment, and in the Progressive Insurance Automotive X PRIZE, Argonne National Laboratory provided dynamometer testing of the super-efficient finalist vehicles. Federal employees with subject matter expertise often serve as members of competition judging panels as well, directly assisting with evaluation and selection of winning solutions. Federal agencies can also identify resources that can be used to promote winning solutions, such as existing communities, networks, websites, forums, and events.

Identifying Participants

Complete a landscape survey. Federal agencies should also consider completing a review of the current companies, research trends, and existing solutions related to the target challenge, either directly or by engaging a partner, vendor, or consultant to complete a report or survey of the business, scientific, and technical landscape related to the target challenge. This step ensures that the target set in the competition is achievable yet sufficiently audacious, and allows agencies to ensure they are not offering a challenge in an area where solutions already exist.

Define outreach plan. Determine who your target audiences are, including solvers, key industry stakeholders, partners, and the media. Establish a communications and outreach plan that goes beyond posting the competition on Challenge.gov to include steps for reaching key audiences, such as through attendance at industry events, webinars, advertising, media outreach, industry association and university networks, etc. Engage the public through online and social media and other complementary programs such as citizen science, education programs, and public voting. The communications and outreach plan for a prize competition should include steps to be taken during each phase of the competition: pre-launch, competition, announcement of winners, and post-competition. Particularly for longer competitions, plan for how to keep enthusiasm and public interest high while the competition is underway prior to the announcement of the winners. Consider how to maintain the enthusiasm and motivation in the community that forms around the competition after the prize is awarded.

At a minimum, agencies should post their competitions on Challenge.gov and must publish a notice in the Federal Register announcing the competition and setting out the rules. Note that even if you are hosting your competition on a website or platform other than Challenge.gov, you can still showcase your challenge on Challenge.gov in a few easy steps. Actively recruit solvers and teams to enter the competition by reaching out to industry and university networks, events, associations, and publications.

Constraining the Solution Space

Identify key program risks and create mitigation plans. Identify key risks to the success of your prize competition and create mitigation plans that will help to reduce any negative impacts of those risks. Common risks in prize competitions include: how to handle too few/many entries; safety plans for physical field testing; enforcement of intellectual property violations; and the potential for no winning solutions.

Developing the Prize

Define competition structure. Once a prize concept has been identified, define the competition structure, including timeline, phases, and stages. Decide if the competition will be single-stage, where submissions are judged once to select winners, or whether it will be multi-stage, with one or more down-select points where entrants are narrowed down to a set of qualified teams, semi-finalists, or finalists. Determine how long each of these phases and stages lasts.

Establish success criteria. Consult with experts in the relevant fields to establish the success metrics/criteria that will be used to select a winner – what does an entrant in the competition have to do to win? These target criteria could be objective and measurable – for example, in the Wendy Schmidt Oil Cleanup X Challenge, winning teams needed to achieve at least 2500 gallons per minute oil recovery rate with at least 70% efficiency of oil to water recovered. Alternately, some competitions use subjective criteria that are assessed by a judging panel – for example, in the Apps for Energy, judges evaluated submissions for their impact, creativity, innovation, and implementation. A combination of objective and subjective criteria can also be used. For multi-stage competitions, each stage may use different criteria for selecting which entrants move forward in the competition.

RESOURCES

HOW can I allocate funding between prize design, administrative costs, and the purse?

WHAT kind of talent do I need to design, advertise, administer, judge, and evaluate a prize?

WHAT partners can provide me with resources and support; attract a useful network of participants; and help build the right brand for my prize?

EVALUATION

WHAT mix of subjective and objective selection criteria will help me incent both creativity and results?

WHAT mechanisms can I use to apply criteria to prize submissions while also building credibility with participants?

HOW can I design rigorous and robust success measures to evaluate whether my prize has achieved its intended outcome more effectively than other strategies I could have used?

MOTIVATORS

WHAT incentives and awards should I offer to attract the right participants to my competition?

HOW can I use my prize to create an environment where participants can compete or collaborate (or both) to achieve a desired outcome?

HOW can I align how I want to use the winning solutions with the intellectual property rights that will attract the right participants?

STRUCTURE

HOW should I develop my eligibility requirements to match the right participants to my problem?

WHAT competition length and features (i.e., segments, rounds, locations) would allow for my prize to achieve my desired outcomes?

HOW can I help participants to make their submissions more innovative and form into communities of interest relevant to my problem?

COMMUNICATIONS

HOW can I develop a marketing plan that targets the right audience segments?

WHAT messages should I create and which media channels reach key stakeholders and participants who have never worked with my organization?

WHAT steps should I take after selecting winners to ensure that my prize has a meaningful impact?

Graphic: Deloitte University Press | DUPress.com[28]

Define judging procedures and validation protocols. Based on the target success criteria you select for each phase of the competition, establish a judging plan. Recruit judges who are experts or influential in the challenge subject area to add authority to the judging. This expertise can come from professional experience, education, or current/prior roles. Consider a mix of judges from different parts of the country and different sectors— including public, private, philanthropic, media, and academia. Judges can also be helpful in promoting the challenge within their networks. Do not select judges who have personal or financial conflicts of interest. Note that the prize authority in America COMPETES exempts judging panels from the Federal Advisory Committee Act (FACA). Establish a judging plan that will allow for each submission to receive review by multiple judges, and include a plan for how to deal with a large number of submissions, in case efforts to recruit entrants are highly successful. In some cases, judging will involve testing a prototype or product in field conditions. Think about when, where, and how to test and validate the performance of the entries, and consider government laboratories and testing facilities that might be applicable.

Determine eligibility. Based on goals for the competition and any restrictions of the authority being used to conduct the competition, decide on what types of individuals and organizations are eligible to compete. Under America COMPETES prize authority, eligibility is limited to U.S.-based companies and U.S. citizens and permanent residents, and Federal entities and Federal employees are not eligible to compete if acting within the scope of their mission or employment.[29] Other authorities may allow international winners. In some competitions, eligibility is limited to particular groups, such as age groups, student status, types of companies, regional/geographic restrictions, or other eligibility requirements.

Define intellectual property provisions. Agencies can consider multiple approaches to intellectual property provisions for prize competitions, upon approval of agency counsel and the signed consent of the submitting participants. Options to consider include leaving ownership of intellectual property in the hands of the solvers, transferring ownership to the government or the public domain, requiring some type of open source license, or providing a license for use (and potentially for derivative works) to the government, among other options.

Identify incentives. Determine the monetary and non-monetary incentives that are available to encourage solvers to enter the competition. To determine the level of monetary prize purse, consider: 1) available budget, 2) prize purses in similar competitions, 3) likely costs for solvers to enter and compete, 4) other market forces, such as cost of current best-of-class products or costs of commercialization, 5) amounts meaningful to attract attention of the media and other key stakeholders, and 6) quantity of prizes to award (such as "seed funding" awards to finalists after an initial competition stage, awards to first, second, and third place winners, or awards to winners in multiple categories. Note that the prize authority in America COMPETES caps the monetary awards at $50,000,000 per prize award. Non-monetary incentives can also motivate teams to compete and include incentives such as: recognition at an awards ceremony or other events; vouchers for access to business consulting, laboratories, or testing resources; media exposure; placement in ads; exposure to a celebrity judging panel or industry experts; commitments to deploy the winning solution in a real-world context post- competition; etc.

Draft competition guidelines and rules. Work with agency general counsel to establish the rules and requirements for the competition, including specifics on competition timeline, incentives (prizes), payment, liability, insurance, how to enter/qualify, submission requirements, eligibility, intellectual property, judging panel, judging process, judging criteria, and other key requirements. In addition to the official rules and legal requirements for the competition, consider creating a plain language summary of the competition timeline, structure, criteria, and judging process, including graphics and images if helpful. Especially for complex, large competitions, consider publishing the draft competition guidelines and rules for a public comment period to allow key stakeholders to raise questions and provide feedback on the competition rules. Create any templates or forms needed for submissions from entrants.

Establish competition operating budget. In addition to funding for the prize purse, prize administration usually requires funding for activities including vendor support; marketing, outreach, collateral, and advertising; travel to key competition events such as competition launch; industry meetings; field testing; an awards ceremony; cost of events; etc.

Select partners and vendors. Identify partners that can support the prize through monetary or non- monetary means. Note that the prize authority in America COMPETES allows for prizes to be co-funded by multiple Federal agencies and by philanthropic and private-sector partners. Identify partners that can contribute key non-monetary resources to the competition, such as testing facilities, data, marketing support, personnel, etc. Identify other Federal agencies with interest in partnering on the funding and administration of the competition given shared goals. Finally, consider selecting a prize design and administration vendor. Some challenge platforms offer specialized solver communities. For example, NASA has used InnoCentive[30] to reach scientists and TopCoder[31] to reach software developers. GSA developed a Schedule for Challenge and Competition Services[32], Schedule 541 4G.

Evaluating Responses and Selecting for Award

When the competition is underway, provide regular updates and encouragement to the solvers that enter the competition. Be responsive to questions and inquiries from solvers. Consider hosting teleconference calls or webinars with entrants to address questions and allow all entrants to participate. While the competition is ongoing, provide regular updates on the process of judging to the entrants and the general public to ensure a transparent process and avoid controversy. When possible, provide reports on progress towards the final competition and judging and, if possible, request updates from the solvers competing for the prize that can be shared with media and the general public. Consider capturing photos, videos, and written anecdotes during the competition, especially during any field testing or in-person events, and keeping mind all relevant privacy considerations. Implement plans to capture impact and evaluation metrics.

Executing the Award

When the competition judging process is complete, publicly announce the top-performing solutions in accordance with the marketing and outreach plan established during competition planning. Present awards to the winning solvers. Payment of prize purses can happen through electronic funds transfer or other means – communicate with agency budget and procurement personnel early to ensure that prize money is distributed in a timely fashion. Host an awards ceremony to recognize the winners. Issue a press release and reach out to general and industry-specific media outlets for coverage of the winners. Consider how to spread the word about the winning solutions intra-agency, inter-agency, and to industry and academia to encourage adoption and scaling of winning solutions. Acknowledge and thank partners that contributed to the prize program.

Involving End Users

After the competition, consider how to spread the word about the winning solutions intra-agency, inter-agency, to local and state governments, and to industry and academia to create lasting impact and encourage adoption and scaling of winning solutions. Create wrap-up and impact reports (including any required reports; see Appendix III for required annual report related to prize authority in America COMPETES).

Managing Risk and Establishing Expectations

Before launching a competition, determine what defines success, identify metrics that can be tracked, and establish a plan for tracking impact. If you are using an online challenge platform to administer your competition, there may be built-in metrics to track certain data, such as the number of participants. Evaluate the effectiveness of your prize program after its completion to inform future program and prize design. Report results within your agency and consider sharing a case study, document template, best practices, and lessons learned with other agency program managers and with the broader prizes community of practice. Consider using impact metrics in outreach to media regarding the results of the competition.

Examples of metrics that can be used to evaluate the effectiveness of a prize program include:

- RETURN ON INVESTMENT (ROI)

- Cost-effectiveness
- Financial leverage
- Time to solution
- SOLUTIONS
  - Quantity of solutions
  - Viability of solutions
  - Diversity of solutions
  - Performance improvement
  - New approaches
- SOLVERS
  - Quantity of entrants
  - Quality/profile of entrants
  - Diversity of entrants
- AWARENESS
  - Earned media impressions
  - Social media impressions
  - Effectiveness of reaching target audiences
  - Stakeholder opinion
- IMPACT
  - Community created/expanded
  - Market adoption
  - Lasting behavior change created

Agencies conducting prize competitions under the authority provided in the America COMPETES Reauthorization Act should complete and submit a report to OSTP at prizes@ostp.gov by the last day in December each year, following the template in Appendix III. Agencies are also encouraged to include in such reports information about prize competitions conducted under other authority. There is no need to report to OSTP if an agency has not conducted any prize competitions during the course of the year.

Providing Technical Guidance and Advice

Share lessons learned in prize design and administration with the prizes community of practice. Continue ongoing communication with the community of stakeholders created during the competition and provide updates about impact in the months and years following the competition.

Pursuing Follow-On Work

Given the structure of this model, follow-on work is not always expected. However, as prize sponsors increase their experience with designing and administering prizes in varied types, scope, and complexity, more prize administrators are using prizes as an integrated piece of an R&D or innovation-focused program, rather than as a stand-alone, one-time initiative. In these innovation portfolios, prizes can be staged or "laddered"—for example, a simple ideation competition could be followed by a technology point-solution competition in which prototypes are built and tested, followed by an exposition or network prize designed at encouraging adoption and scaling of demonstrated solutions. In these portfolio programs, successful prize administrators treat the communities and networks of people that form around these competitions as ongoing assets, investing in communications, outreach, and events to maintain interest, enthusiasm, and knowledge-sharing in the community.

Prize Successes

There are numerous instances of agency successes using prize authority:

- **Astronaut Glove Challenge**: Before entrepreneur Peter Homer and his startup spacesuit company Flagsuit LLC[33] won NASA's $450,000 prize purse in 2009 for designing a flexible glove better than those in use by NASA's astronauts, he had been a satellite designer, sailmaker, microgravity experiment designer, and local community center director. Since winning the competition, Flagsuit LLC has continued to grow, obtaining contracts with Orbital Outfitters in 2007 to supply gloves for their Industrial Suborbital Spacesuit being manufactured for XCOR and signing a sole source, prime contract in 2011 with NASA to develop and test improved spacesuit glove assemblies. http://www.nasa.gov/offices/oct/early_stage_innovation/centennial_c hallenges/astronaut_glove/i ndex.html
- **Wendy Schmidt Oil Cleanup X Challenge**: The $1.4 million 2011 competition, supported by technical expertise from the Department of Interior and NOAA, inspired entrepreneurs, engineers, and scientists worldwide to develop innovative, rapidly deployable, and highly efficient methods of cleaning up oil spills from the ocean surface. The winner, Elastec/American Marine[34] – a growing Illinois-based manufacturer of oil spill and environmental equipment that uses local

talent for nearly all its fabrication – recovered oil at a rate more than three times the best previously recorded in controlled conditions. http://www.iprizecleanoceans.org/

- **Vehicle Stopper Challenge**: This 2011 Air Force Research Laboratory (AFRL) competition focused on a problem that had vexed military security forces and civilian police for years: how to safely stop uncooperative fleeing vehicles without causing permanent damage to the vehicle or harm any of the occupants. Through this competition, AFRL was able to multiply the number of people thinking about this problem over 100-fold and received a workable solution within a 60-day period. For a $25,000 purse, a retired 66-year-old mechanical engineer from Lima, Peru submitted the winning solution. http://www.msnbc.msn.com/id/44994706/ns/technology_and_science-innovation/t/air-force- innovation-prizes-make-cents-budget-era/

- **Progressive Insurance Automotive X Prize**: This 2010 competition, sponsored in part by the Department of Energy (DOE), awarded $10 million in prizes in 2010 to three teams that built production-capable, super fuel-efficient vehicles that exceeded 100 MPG or the energy equivalent. 111 teams from around the globe developed a new generation of technologies as well as a goldmine of technical data from on-track and laboratory testing. For example, the Virginia team that won one of the three prizes used a fuel-injected internal combustion engine, but focused on building a super light car that boasts the lowest drag coefficient of any car ever tested in the GM wind tunnel. In contrast, another winner from North Carolina built an electric car powered by a best-in-class lithium-ion battery and 91.5% efficient battery charger. The winning approaches were identified through objective evaluation using clear performance metrics. The prize's sponsors and the industry at large benefited from a gold mine of publicly available technical data collected from test track and laboratory conditions on the competing technologies under rigorous conditions. http://www.progressiveautoxprize.org/

- **Data-Driven Forecasting of Solar Events Challenge**: This NASA challenge for a predictive algorithm to help protect America's astronauts from radiation exposure in space inspired over 500 problem solvers from 53 countries. NASA received a solution that exceeded their requirements from a retired radio-frequency engineer in rural

New Hampshire, Bruce Cragin. Cragin's winning approach forecast solar proton events 8 hours in advance with 85% accuracy, a result NASA dubbed "outstanding." In fact, in a survey[35] of the nearly 3000 solvers that competed in seven NASA prizes, 81% reported that they had never before responded to a government request for proposals, let alone worked with NASA.
https://www.innocentive.com/ar/challenge/9059496

Additional success stories can be found in Appendix II, Public-Sector Prize Examples.

Conclusion

In summary, prizes are now a standard tool for open innovation in every Federal agency's toolbox. Specifically, prizes enable the Federal government to pay only for success, establish an ambitious goal, and reach beyond the "usual suspects" to increase the number of minds tackling a problem without having to predict which team or approach is most likely to succeed. Incentive prizes are one type of "pull mechanism" – results-based market incentives designed to overcome market failures and catalyze innovation. There are a variety of different prize types that can achieve different types of goals, including: exemplar, point-solution, market stimulation, exposition, participation, and network prizes. Many well-known incentive prizes have focused on catalyzing technology R&D, though prize administrators are increasingly using incentive prizes to drive behavior change, market adoption of existing solutions and interventions, and progress in areas of social policy such as health, energy use, economic development, and education. In December 2010, Congress passed the America COMPETES Reauthorization Act, providing all Federal agencies broad authority to conduct prize competitions as called for by the President.

The first step in designing a successful incentive prize is to engage in problem definition to identify a problem or opportunity that meaningfully impacts program goals, mission, and strategy and that can feasibly be addressed in part or in whole through an incentive prize. Once a challenge has been identified, agencies should work with partners, experts, and key stakeholders to deconstruct the problem, complete a landscape survey of current research trends and solutions, and identify resources such as datasets, testing facilities, and expertise. During competition planning, agencies should define a competition structure; establish target success criteria; secure a prize purse and other incentives; finalize prize rules, outreach plan, and budget; and identify and select partners and vendors. During the competition, agencies should support communications with solvers, key stakeholders, and the general public and should ensure a fair judging process. After the winners have been announced, agencies should take steps to ensure the winning solutions are implemented and scaled and that the community created around the competition becomes an ongoing asset.

Agencies are encouraged to evaluate the effectiveness of prize program to inform future program and prize design, report results, and consider best practices and lessons learned with the prizes community of practice.

APPENDIX I. RESOURCES FOR PRIZE ADMINISTRATORS AT FEDERAL AGENCIES

News Coverage of Public Sector Prizes

- Forbes: "Incentivizing Innovation: How The White House Uses Challenge.gov To Solve Big Problems" (February 2014)
  http://www. forbes.com/sites/rahimkanani/2014/02/17/incentivizing-innovation-how-the- white-house-uses-challenge-gov-to-solve-big-problems/
- Information Week: "GSA's Challenge.gov Wins Harvard Innovation Award" (January 2014)
  http://www.informationweek.com/government/leadership/gsas-challengegov-wins-harvard- innovation-award/d/d-id/1113559
- Los Angeles Times: "Scientific Research Increasingly Fueled by Prize Money" (January 2013) http://articles.latimes.com/2013/jan/10/science/la-sci-funding-competition-20130110
- USA Today: "White House touts 'challenge' prizes for tech solutions" (April 2012)
  http://www.usatoday.com/tech/news/story/2012-04-09/white-house-challenges- technology/54136706/1?csp=34news
- CNET: "How the White House is aiming the X Prize model at big problems" (June 2012)
  http://news.cnet.com/8301-11386_3-57450870-76/how-the-white-house-is-aiming-the-x-prize- model-at-big-problems/

- NY Times Opinionator: "Innovation for the People, by the People" (February 2012) http://opinionator.blogs.nytimes.com/2012/02/22/from-the-white-house-incentives-to- innovate/
- NPR Planet Money Blog on historical prize examples (March 2012) http://www.npr.org/blogs/money/2012/03/01/147751097/why-napoleon-offered-a-prize-for- inventing-canned-food?sc=fb&cc=fp
- Freakonomics/Vijay Vaitheeswaran Blog: "The Rise of the Prize" (March 2012) http://www.freakonomics.com/2012/03/14/the-rise-of-the-prize/

OSTP Reports and Blogs

- Initial Report from OSTP to Congress on Prizes and America COMPETES in FY2011 (March 2012) http://www.whitehouse.gov/sites/default/files/microsites/ostp/competes_report_on_prizes_fi nal.pdf
- Implementation of Federal Prize Authority: Fiscal Year 2012 Progress Report (December 2013) http://www.whitehouse.gov/sites/default/files/microsites/ostp/competes_prizesreport_dec-2013.pdf
- Implementation of Federal Prize Authority: Fiscal Year 2013 Progress Report (May 2014) http://www.whitehouse.gov/sites/default/files/microsites/ostp/competes_prizesreport_fy13_fi nal.pdf
- Identifying Steps Forward in Use of Prizes to Spur Innovation (April 10, 2012, OSTP Blog) http://www.whitehouse.gov/blog/2012/04/10/identifying-steps-forward-use-prizes-spur- innovation
- Unleashing Innovation and Deepening Democracy Through Prizes (June 12, 2012, White House Blog) http://www.whitehouse.gov/blog/2012/06/12/unleashing-innovation-deepening-democracy- through-prizes
- Challenge.gov: Two Years and 200 Prizes Later (September 5, 2012, OSTP Blog) http://www.whitehouse.gov/blog/2012/09/05/challengegov-two-years-and-200-prizes-later

OMB and White House Guidance

- Open Government Directive (December 8, 2009)
  - http://www.whitehouse.gov/sites/default/files/omb/assets/memora nda_2010/m10-06.pdf
  - "[Agency Open Government Plans should include] innovative methods, such as prizes and competitions, to obtain ideas from and to increase collaboration with those in the private sector, non-profit, and academic communities."
- 2009 Strategy for American Innovation (September 2009)
  - http://www.whitehouse.gov/sites/default/files/microsites/ostp/inn ovation- whitepaper.pdf
  - "The Federal government should take advantage of the expertise and insight of people both inside and outside the Federal government, use high-risk, high-reward policy tools such as prizes and challenges to solve tough problems..."
- Updated Strategy for American Innovation (February 2011, see box 2, page 12):
  http://www.whitehouse.gov/sites/default/files/uploads/InnovationStrat egy.pdf
- Guidance on the Use of Challenges and Prizes to Promote Open Government (March 8, 2010):
  http://www.whitehouse.gov/sites/default/files/omb/assets/memoranda _2010/m10-11.pdf
- Fact Sheet and FAQ on Prize Authority in the America COMPETES Reauthorization Act (2011):
  https://cio.gov/wp-   content/uploads/downloads/2012/09/Prize_ Authority_in_the_America_COMPETES_Reauthoriz ation_Act.pdf
- FAQ on PRA & Prizes and Challenges (March 1, 2012):
  http://www.whitehouse.gov/sites/default/files/omb/assets/inforeg/chal lenge-and-prizes- faqs.pdf

General Services Administration

- Challenge.gov (over 200 challenges from more than 45 agencies and departments):
  http://www.challenge.gov/

- HowTo.gov information on best practices of prize design and administration:
  http://www.howto.gov/social-media/challenges
- GSA Schedule 541-G – "Challenges and Competitions Services" vendors on schedule:
  http://www.gsaelibrary.gsa.gov/ElibMain/sinDetails.do?scheduleNum ber=541&specialItemNum ber=541+4G&executeQuery=YES
- PRA Guidance – GSA's guidance regarding the relation between the Paperwork Reduction Act and challenge.gov:
  http://www.howto.gov/sites/default/files/Challengegov-and-the-Paperwork- Reduction-Act.pdf
- PII Guidance – GSA's guidance regarding the relation between privacy issues, personally- identifiable information (PII) and challenge.gov:
  http://www.howto.gov/sites/default/files/documents/ChallengegovPri vacyPrimer.pdf
- Security Guidance – GSA's guidance regarding the security of challenge.gov to host challenges:
  http://www.howto.gov/sites/default/files/documents/ChallengegovSec urityPrimer.pdf
- Children's Privacy Guidance – GSA's guidance regarding the protection of young users participating in challenges on challenge.gov:
  http://www.howto.gov/sites/default/files/documents/ChallengegovCO PPAandYoungUserPrime r.pdf
- Cookie Guidance – GSA's guidance regarding the use of persistent cookies safely to enhance user's experience on challenge.gov:
  http://www.howto.gov/sites/default/files/documents/ChallengegovCo okiesPrimer.pdf

NASA Center of Excellence for Collaborative Innovation

- Virtual Center of Excellence for Collaborative Innovation:
  http://www.nasa.gov/offices/COECI/index.html
- New Center of Excellence Fuels Prize to Help Modernize Tools for Patent Examination (December 16, 2011, OSTP Blog):
  http://www.whitehouse.gov/blog/2011/12/16/new-center-excellence-fuels-prize-help- modernize-tools-patent-examination

Agency-Specific Guidance

- HHS: Resources for Challenge Managers at HHS and HHS delegation of authority
- NASA: NASA Policy Directive on Challenges, Prize Competitions, and Crowdsourcing Activities

Other

- McKinsey 2009 report "And the Winner Is...": http://mckinseyonsociety.com/downloads/reports/Social-Innovation/And_the_winner_is.pdf
- Deloitte University Press report "The Craft of Prize Design: Lessons learned from the public sector" http://www.nesta.org.uk/sites/default/files/challenge_prize_design_practice_guide_0.pdf
- NESTA's "Challenge Prizes: A Practice guide": http://www.nesta.org.uk/sites/default/files/challenge_prize_design_practice_guide_0.pdf
- Harvard Berkman Center for Internet & Society 2012 paper on "Public-Private Partnerships for Organizing and Executing Prize-Based Competitions": http://cyber.law.harvard.edu/publications/2012/public_private_partnerships_for_organizing_a nd_executing_prize-based_competitions
- June 2012 Collaborative Innovation conference on public sector prizes (video of panel sessions, presentation decks from the event, and links to relevant reports): http://www.casefoundation.org/collaborative-innovation

APPENDIX II. PUBLIC-SECTOR PRIZE EXAMPLES

- **Mapping Dark Matter Competition**: NASA, the European Space Agency, the Royal Astronomical Society, and Kaggle teamed up to launch a data-mining competition tackling a problem that physicists have been working on for decades: mapping "dark matter." In less than a week, Martin O'Leary, a PhD student in glaciology, had crafted an algorithm that outperformed the state-of-the- art algorithms most commonly used in astronomy for mapping dark matter. O'Leary applied techniques[36] used in his field such as detecting edges in glacier fronts from satellite images. Ultimately, 73 teams submitted a total of 760 entries as they vied for first place. The winners – a cosmology professor and grad student team from the University of California, Irvine – submitted 16 times, continuously improving their statistical model with feedback from a live leaderboard to emerge on top. Beyond O'Leary, fierce competition continued to emerge from unexpected places, including from a neuroscientist at Harvard Medical School and a signature verification expert at Qatar University whose research brings quantitative modeling techniques[37] to the understanding of flowing Arabic script. The participants invested significant time and thought motivated by a very modest prize: an expense paid trip to NASA's Jet Propulsion Laboratory in California to present their ideas to NASA scientists.

http://www.kaggle.com/c/mdm

- **Shredder Challenge**: Following the success of the DARPA Urban Challenge[38] that demonstrated dramatic leaps forward in the capabilities of autonomous vehicles, DARPA's 2011 Shredder Challenge called upon computer scientists and puzzle enthusiasts to compete for up to $50,000 by piecing together a series of shredded documents. The prize's goal was to identify and assess potential capabilities that could be used by our warfighters operating in war zones, but that might also create vulnerabilities to sensitive information that is protected through our own shredding practices throughout the U.S. national security community. Almost 9,000 teams registered to participate in DARPA's Shredder Challenge and 33 days after the challenge was announced, one small San Francisco-based team correctly solved the puzzles. The winning team spent nearly 600 man-hours developing algorithms and piecing together documents that were shredded into more than 10,000 pieces. DARPA stated that experts had been skeptical that a solution could be produced at all, let alone in such a short time frame.

http://www.darpa.mil/NewsEvents/Releases/2011/12/02_.aspx

- **FTC Robocall Challenge:** In April 2013, the Federal Trade Commission (FTC) announced the winners of its Robocall Challenge, the agency's first public prize competition. The FTC receives about 200,000 complaints each month regarding these harassing calls.

That's why the FTC announced the Robocall Challenge in October 2012, with a $50,000 prize for the individual or small group that could come up with the best technical proposal to help consumers block illegal robocalls. "Nomorobo" is one of the winning solutions – developed by citizen solver Aaron Foss, this service allows incoming calls to be routed to a second telephone line that can identify and hang up on illegal robocalls before they could ring through to users. Nomorobo now has over 25,000 users and is protecting more than 18,000 phone lines from over 48,000 robocalls per week. Aaron emphasizes that he never would have worked on the robocall problem if not for the FTC's open challenge.

http://robocall.challenge.gov/

- **DTRA Algorithm Challenge:** In 2013, the Defense Threat Reduction Agency (DTRA) offered a $1M prize for innovative algorithms for the individual or team that could develop an algorithm which can most rapidly and accurately characterize a complex clinical sample – a very difficult algorithmic challenge. Almost 3,000 solvers participated in the competition and more than 65 solvers submitted solutions. 24 solutions were able to pass the threshold for 90% accuracy, and the winning team, Team Huson, was able to do so in less than 10 minutes – a 100x improvement over existing tools. "Team Huson's solution to the challenge will lead to an enhancement of DTRA's capability to diagnose and treat biothreats to the U.S. Armed Forces by giving DoD the ability to process and analyze biological sequence data rapidly in a realistic, moderate-to-low resource setting," said Dr. Christian Whitchurch, Devices Branch Manager for DTRA's Diagnostics, Detection and Disease Surveillance Division.

http://www.prweb.com/releases/dtra/algorithmchallenge/prweb11150
852.htm

- **Apps for Energy**: The Department of Energy offered $100,000 in prizes to software developers for the best new applications (apps) that help utility customers make the most out of their Green Button electricity usage data. The Grand Prize winner, Leafully, helps people understand energy usage by diving deep into hourly data with historic trends, understanding the effect of the abstract units of energy, and taking action along with friends.

http://appsforenergy.challenge.gov/

- **Census Return Rate Challenge**: The U.S. Census Bureau conducted a prize competition that challenged statisticians, mathematicians, and other data scientists to analyze Census data in order to create a statistical model to predict Decennial Census mail return rates at the Census block group level of geography. The winning teams' models used statistical methods not previously utilized by the agency and will be used in modeling for the decennial census and demographic sample surveys.
  http://www.kaggle.com/c/us-census-challenge
- **My Air, My Health Challenge**: With $160K in prizes offered by the U.S. Environmental Protection Agency (EPA) and the U.S. Department of Health and Human Service (HHS), this competition was a multidisciplinary call to innovators to create a personal, portable, near-real-time, location-specific system to monitor and report air pollutants and potentially related health events. Judges unanimously awarded the $100,000 prize to the team of David Kuller, Gabrielle Dockterman, and Dot Kelly for their Conscious Clothing prototype. Built to scale, this system could cost as little as $20. Its affordable price, comfort, and near-invisibility make it attractive not only to researchers and communities, but to individuals looking to take charge of their own health.
  http://challenge.gov/HHS/372-my-air-my-health-challenge?sso=f45
  befb720f7653bf9d96119735d37b6207d9827c1a8d136c2e423274a234
  bd6cac6a7822fbdc774a771073f4de4c047bdbd
- **Challenge to Identify Audacious Goals in Vision Research and Blindness Rehabilitation**: This open ideation competition offered $100K for the identification of audacious goals relevant to the National Eye Institute's mission to stimulate innovation in national vision research. The winners were invited to present their ideas at a 2013 NEI gathering of more than 200 experts working to develop a set of bold goals that will guide vision research priorities for the NEI going forward. NEI received 476 entries in the competition from across the country. Almost half of the submissions came from people who had never received NIH research funding. Dr. Paul Sieving, director of the NEI at the National Institutes of Health, stated: "the buzz that surrounded the challenge was very effective in attracting input from leading researchers, engineers, philanthropists, patient advocates, and venture capitalists, many of whom had not previously received NIH funding. The competition allowed us to reach out to

everyone in the Nation—even those not engaged in vision research."
http://challenge.gov/NIH/390-challenge-to-identify-audacious-goals-
in-vision-research-and- blindness-rehabilitation

- **Mozilla Ignite Challenge**: In this $500K multi-stage competition,
  Mozilla and the National Science Foundation (NSF) invited designers,
  developers and everyday people to brainstorm and build applications
  for the faster, smarter Internet of the future. The winning entries were
  designed to run on next-generation networks with speeds of up to one
  gigabit per second — roughly 250 times faster than the internet most
  of us are used to today. The twenty-two winning entries included
  applications that would aid emergency responders, enable three-
  dimensional video conferencing, provide real-time health monitoring,
  and inform connected traffic control systems, among other ideas.
  "These winning apps offer a glimpse into how we might catalyze the
  innovation ecosystem to develop next-generation applications and
  services with enormous public benefit," said Farnam Jahanian, the
  head of NSF's Directorate for Computer and Information Science and
  Engineering. http://challenge.gov/NSF/380-mozilla-ignite

- **Investing in Innovation (i2)**: Led by the Office of the National
  Coordinator for Health Information Technology (ONC), the core of
  the $5 million i2 program is a series of prize competitions – up to 15
  each year – to accelerate innovation and adoption of Health
  Information Technology (Health IT) for improved clinical outcomes
  and efficient care delivery.

  Under i2, the National Cancer Institute (NCI) partnered with ONC to
  launch the "Using Public Data for Cancer Prevention and Control:
  From Innovation to Impact" competition[39] in July 2011. HHS's
  competition challenged software development teams to use public
  data to build an application to promote healthy behaviors for cancer
  prevention (e.g., nutrition, physical activity, or smoking cessation),
  aid early detection and screening, inform decision-making, or increase
  patient adherence to treatment plans. The second place $20,000 prize
  was awarded to My Cancer Genome[40], an application that leverages
  the NCI Physician Data Query (PDQ) dataset to provide – for the first
  time – tailored decision support for treatment options based on tumor
  gene mutations. The team lead for My Cancer Genome, Dr. Mia Levy,
  was able to bring a rare combination of expertise in clinical oncology,
  genomic medicine, and bioinformatics to bear on the NCI/ONC
  challenge. Dr. Levy serves as a clinical faculty member at Vanderbilt.

Yet, she previously failed to secure traditional National Institutes of Health funding for the My Cancer Genome application because of its focus on the translation and application of existing scientific evidence for clinical impact. The challenge provided a rapid mechanism for her team to gain publicity and support for further development of an important, emerging area of cancer treatment decision support. Dr. Levy has gone on to get an SBIR grant. She also received $100K from GE in commercialization support[41] after placing second in the HHS challenge.

In another i2-supported competition, Axial Exchange[42] from North Carolina won first prize in December 2011 in the U.S. Department of Health and Human Office of the National Coordinator's "Ensuring Safe Transitions from Hospital to Home" Challenge.[43] The Challenge asked developers to create solutions that improve patient safety and facilitate care transitions for patients discharged from hospitals to other care settings (including but not limited to homes, nursing homes and hospices). Axial Exchange's winning solution, The Axial Care Transition Suite, is a web-based application that enables information to flow to a patient's next care setting so that providers have what they need, when they need it, and so that patients are engaged with the information and tools needed to improve their health knowledge and enhance their ownership of after-care responsibilities. In June 2012, Axial Exchange announced that it had acquired mRemedy – a company formed in 2009 by DoApp, Inc. and Mayo Clinic – to offer a mobile healthcare platform to healthcare providers. The acquisition provides Axial Exchange with software and customers that will complement Axial Exchange's award-winning care transition products. Canaan Partners, Axial's lead venture capital investor, and Mayo Clinic both invested in Axial Exchange to complete the deal. http://www.healthit.gov/policy-researchers-implementers/health-it-prizes-challenges

- **Blue Button® for All Americans Prize Contest**: The Veterans Administration (VA) sponsored this 2011 competition to help veterans have access to their heath information regardless of where they get their care. This challenge asked HealthIT software developers to include a Blue Button data download function in personal health records (PHR) systems and then arrange to install the PHR on patient-facing websites of 25,000 doctors across America. The Blue Button is a tool that gives patients access to their personal health data via an electronic file that is easy to read by both people and computers. The winner of the $50,000 prize – McKesson Corporation's Relay Health division – added Blue Button download functions to its existing PHR system which is used by approximately 200,000 doctors and 2,000 hospitals. McKesson donated the cash prize to the Wounded Warrior Project after being declared the winner of the challenge in October 2011.

While typical contract and grant making development cycles span several months before soliciting proposals, this challenge took only six weeks to develop and launch. VA was able to declare a winner of the challenge approximately four months after the announcement date: this time included about four weeks of evaluation of the winner's entry. VA estimates that performance periods under a contract or grant would have been at least three times as long. Had the winner merely installed a Blue Button-enabled PHR in the patient portals of 25,000 doctors – the minimum necessary – the $50,000 prize would equate to a cost of two dollars per doctor. Because the winner added the Blue Button function to the PHRs used by the approximately 200,000 doctors in its system, the prize amount cost the taxpayers about 25 cents per doctor. The winner's user base had substantially more than the 25,000 minimum doctors required, and in addition represented a very significant share of the overall doctor and hospital markets: almost a third of America's practicing doctors and slightly more than a third of the country's registered hospitals.

https://www.myhealth.va.gov/index.html

APPENDIX III: TEMPLATE FOR ANNUAL REPORT TO WHITE HOUSE OSTP & CONGRESS

Submission Details

- **Submit reports by email to**: prizes@ostp.gov **for the prior fiscal year by the last day of the calendar year.**
- **Requirements:** Section 24(p) of the Stevenson-Wydler Act requires a report on all prize competitions conducted under Section 2. Agencies should use the template below to report to OSTP all activities under section 24. Agencies are also encouraged to report to OSTP on prize

competitions conducted under other legal authorities, including why the competition was conducted under that authority.

- **Clearance:** In your submission, please confirm that appropriate agency leadership has approved the report.

Report Template

This template is to be completed separately for each prize, competition, or challenge, including prizes launched, underway, or completed during the fiscal year.

1. **Title** of prize competition or challenge
2. **Sponsoring Agency**
3. **Primary Point of Contact** for the prize competition (name, email address, and phone number)
4. **Tagline** of 350 words or less. Similar to the first line of a newspaper story, the tagline should clearly explain what the prize competition is, who the prize challenged, what it challenged them to do, and why it is important or unique.
5. **Link** to the homepage for the prize competition (e.g., link on Challenge.gov)
6. **Problem Statement.** Explain the problem or opportunity the prize competition is designed to address. What specifically were participants in the competition asked to do or submit in order to be eligible to win the competition? What were the target requirements and success criteria for selection of a winner or winners?
7. **Proposed Goals.** What were the primary objectives of the prize competition?
8. **Why a Prize.** Provide an analysis of why a prize competition was the preferable method of achieving the goals described in #7 as opposed to other authorities available to the agency, such as contracts, grants, and cooperative agreements.
9. **Participants.** Whom did the agency hope to mobilize to compete? What were the competition's eligibility requirements? If registration has opened for the competition, provide a summary of the quantity of entrants to date if available. If the competition has completed, provide a summary of the quantity of entrants into the competition, along with a descriptive summary of the aggregate profile of those entrants – for

example, team size (individuals, companies, or teams), geographic distribution, or other notable attributes of the entrant pool.

10. **Timeline.** When was the competition launched? What were the dates of key milestones and events during the competition (such as phases or submission deadlines)? What is (or was) the competition's completion date?

11. **Solicitation & Outreach.** What methods did the agency use to market the prize competition, mobilize potential participants, and ensure high quality submissions? What methods are or will be utilized to raise awareness of the competition and its results with other audiences such as the general public? Were those methods effective? Did the agency learn any lessons about outreach that might be valuable for future prize competitions?

12. **Incentives.** What incentives did the agency provide for participants to compete in the prize competition (monetary and non-monetary)? What is the total amount of cash prizes awarded for the prize competition, including a description of the amount of any private funds contributed for prize purses and the sources of those private funds? What is the manner in which the amounts of cash prizes awarded and claimed were allocated among the accounts of the agency for recording as obligations and expenditures (i.e., what amount(s) were obligated to what appropriations account(s))? What non- monetary incentives were used to motivate participants and reward winners?

13. **Evaluation and Judging.** What methods did the agency use to judge and evaluate submissions to the prize competition? Were those methods effective? Did the agency learn any lessons about judging and evaluation that might be valuable for future prize competitions?

14. **Partnerships.** What partnerships did your agency form (formal or informal) with other agencies or private sector entities (including philanthropic organizations) to make successful a prize competition conducted under section 24? What were the benefits derived from those partnerships (such as in-kind support, monetary contributions, or marketing and outreach)? Did the agency learn any lessons about public-private partnerships that might be valuable for future prize competitions?

15. **Resources.** Which agency resources, including personnel and funding, did the agency use in the execution of each prize competition? Please provide a detailed description of the activities for

which those resources were used and an accounting of how funding for execution was allocated among the accounts of the agency for recording as obligations and expenditures (i.e., amounts in personnel and other administrative expenses associated with the prize competition that were obligated and spent under each relevant appropriations account).

16. **Results.** Please explain how the prize competition advanced the mission of the agency and the specific objectives identified in #7. Impact and advancement of agency mission could be measured in multiple ways that vary based on the goals and objectives of the competition. Examples of objective and subjective success criteria include dollars saved, quantity or diversity of ideas or approaches, quantity or diversity of participants, the novel or elegant nature of solutions, or quantity of traditional and social media impressions, among others. *Information and anecdotes about the winners and winning solutions of the competition are particularly of interest.* If the competition is still underway, provide an initial assessment of the impact of the prize competition to date.

CHALLENGE BASED ACQUISITIONS: TRY BEFORE YOU BUY

What Are Challenge-Based Acquisitions?

Challenges (or incentive prizes) are most frequently used to draw attention to excellence, spur market development, or encourage industry networking.[44] Challenge-based acquisition takes the government- endorsed challenge concept[45] a step further by making it part of the procurement process, bringing the innovation opportunity of a challenge into the procurement framework of the Federal Acquisition Regulation (FAR). This allows the government to use challenges as the core of its evaluations, pay vendors for participation, and most importantly, test and purchase quantities beyond simply prototypes. It is a mechanism to:

- Communicate needed capability,
- Encourage innovation in a minimally prescriptive environment,

- Assess candidate offerings, and
- Purchase proven solutions.

For more detailed information about Challenge-Based Acquisitions, see the handbook and symposium proceedings cited below.[46,47]

Basic Steps of Challenge-Based Acquisition

Understand Acquisition Objectives

Understand what is needed in terms of a missing capability or an unsatisfied gap in a current capability. This understanding should be expressible using concepts and terms from the capability domain. It should focus on what is needed and not how the need should be resolved. This is not a license to be vague. Expression of a sought capability can be very detailed and specific but should avoid specifying a solution. Statements of sought capability that stray into the specification of a solution can constrain industry and limit innovation.

Design the Challenge

The challenge should be transparent and understandable. It should let challengers prove that their solution is the capability sought by the government. This forces the government to design a challenge that, if met, proves that the offered solution provides the needed capability.

Plan the Contract

The purpose of challenge-based acquisition is to acquire a solution that provides a needed capability. Evidence gained from a challenge is part of a source-selection process or part of an evaluation process leading to a production buy. This requires rigor and thoughtful contract planning so that fairness and transparency are maintained. Industry will be incentivized to participate so long as the potential to win a production contract award is present.

Communicate Capability Needs

A challenge in support of acquisition fails if potential challengers are unaware of it. The government can use a wealth of outlets to advertise its intent to hold a challenge. No matter which outlets are chosen, the government message has at its heart a challenge description. Industry learns what capability the government needs through the challenge description and is stimulated to devise innovative solutions.

Establish an Initial Pool

Determine the set of challengers that will be invited to participate in the first challenge event. Choosing the initial pool size is a balance between the desire to maximize challenger participation, and thus competition, versus the cost of challenge execution. Initial pool admission can be based on something as simple as a white paper stating relevant experience or technical approach to the challenge.

Conduct the Challenge Event

Challenge events should be conducted with scientific rigor. Evidence collected at an event should be of sufficient quality to inform acquisition decisions.

Evaluate Challenge Results

Evidence collected during challenge event execution must be evaluated to determine whether the needed capability was demonstrated. This is not necessarily a discrete decision. The field of challengers may show progress in the direction of capability satisfaction yet not reach the stated evaluation criteria. If so, the government may choose to offer the challenge again, modify the challenge, or quit.

Reduce the Challenger Pool

If it can be determined that a particular challenger is not likely to benefit from further participation in the challenge and that their prospective solution does not or will not fulfill the capability need, that challenger should be eliminated from further consideration. Such a decision can save money for both government and industry. As such, contracting strategies for a Challenge-Based Acquisition should include provisions to off-ramp non-performers.

Procure Solutions

If the evaluation of evidence from one or more challengers is satisfactory and proper contracting procedures were observed, the government can and should purchase the winning solution.

Government Role

In traditional acquisition, the government communicates its needs in a specification, assuming that fulfillment of the specification equates to meeting mission needs. However, the specification could be under-constrained, over-constrained, or simply wrong. Any of these conditions can result in the project going longer, costing more than anticipated or being unachievable. It is important to recognize that the specification may unduly drive the design and possibly limit the government's ability to obtain the best outcome. To avoid these problems and implement challenge-based acquisition successfully, the government must allow industry to innovate within a well-defined outcome based framework. To do this the government should consider the following:

Innovate

Challenge-based acquisition requires government program managers and contracting officers to foster innovation within their organizations – to identify and implement innovative approaches like challenge- based acquisition, to improve performance, shorten schedules, and reduce costs. The FAR permits challenge-based acquisition as a type of business process innovation:

> The absence of direction should be interpreted as permitting the team to innovate and use sound business judgment that is otherwise consistent with law and within the limits of their authority. Contracting officers should take the lead in encouraging business process innovations and ensuring that business decisions are sound.[48]

Decompose Complex Requirements Into Challenges

The government must interpret user requirements and translate them into meaningful challenge events that give industry the latitude for innovation and get users what they need. This requires the government to have a broad vision and a commitment to success beyond that typically needed to issue a Request for Proposal or Broad Agency Announcement. Further, the government must ensure that technical details are not over-specified, but rather generalized into technology-agnostic capability requirements that can be demonstrated in a challenge.

Generalize User Experience and Needs then Communicate Them to Industry

After gathering requirements from the user and translating them into executable challenges, the government must communicate the scope of the challenges to industry. In doing so, the government assumes risk, because formulating the challenges requires interpreting and translating user experience and needs in a clear and concise manner.

Find Unclassified Analogues to Classified Situations

The government can employ challenge-based acquisition to identify solutions to classified requirements by utilizing unclassified challenge analogues. In these situations, participants may not know the details of the particular setting in which the government plans to use a solution, but would only know the general performance objectives to be met. This approach supports an enhanced competitive environment by including vendors who do not have appropriate security clearances and facilities.

Design and Execute Concrete Challenge Apparatus

The government must design challenge-specific execution and evaluation processes that include:

- A plan for communicating challenges to industry,
- A plan detailing how the challenge will be executed contractually,
- Specific requirements for challenge participation, and
- Detailed evaluation criteria to ensure the challenge evaluation is fair to all participants.

Perform Quantitative and Qualitative Analysis of Challenge Results

The government must use rigorous quantitative and qualitative measurements to evaluate challenge results. Upon completion of the challenge, the government may elect to:

- Purchase one or more of the competitor offerings based on product utility demonstrated during the challenge.
- Refine and reissue the challenge based on lessons learned during challenge performance. This can become part of an incremental government strategy that includes challenge-based research projects.

- Do nothing. If the challenge results did not inspire confidence that any of the products would meet government needs, the government has no obligation to procure a product.

Industry Role

Industry also takes on a new role in challenge-based acquisition: one that more closely mirrors how industry normally develops and brings a product to the commercial market. In the commercial marketplace, industry independently develops a solution to address a given capability need. This approach contrasts with the traditional federal acquisition process where industry responds to the government-provided set of detailed specifications and requirements. In the former case, industry bears most of the risk, while in the latter case the government bears the risk. Thus, in support of challenge-based acquisition, industry must consider the following:

Innovate
Challenge-based acquisition does not presuppose one specific, technological solution. This demands that industry propose innovative solutions. Consequently, the government must not prescribe a specific technological path that industry must follow, but rather present its requirements in the form of general challenge objectives that must be met. Industry then applies its expertise to determine the best technical approach to meet the objectives within the schedule and cost constraints provided by the government.

Cooperate with Traditional and Non-Traditional Entities
No company has a monopoly on innovative solutions. Challenge-based acquisition seeks the best technology to address government needs. Therefore, industry must be willing to cooperate with individuals or organizations that could contribute to developing a successful solution.

Dedicate Independent Research and Development (IR&D) Funding
Challenge-based acquisition encourages industry to dedicate its own IR&D funds, defined in FAR 31.001 and 31.205-18(a), to develop solutions that meet challenge performance criteria. While the government may choose to fund organizations to participate in challenge events, it may choose not to fund any of their initial development effort.

Negotiate Intellectual Property Licenses

Challenge-based acquisition requires that industry be prepared to negotiate potential intellectual property licenses with the government. As a result, industry must identify which of its solutions are derived through exclusive use of IR&D funding versus those developed at partial or full government expense. Such a distinction is important because the source of funding dictates the type of licensing rights available to the government.

Successes

Culvert Denial Challenge

In August 2014, the Joint Improvised Explosive Device Defeat Organization (JIEDDO) awarded a multiple award IDIQ contract for the JIEDDO Culvert Denial Challenge. Through this IDIQ, the government seeks innovative technical solutions for surveillance and inspection of Improvised Explosive Device (IED) emplacements in and around culverts. Ten vendors will participate in a Surveillance Challenge event and another 10 vendors will participate in an Inspection Challenge event. The 20 vendors will compete on a Ft. Benning, GA training range in October 2014.

2012 Counter-IED Robotics Challenge

The JIEDDO Counter-IED Robotics Challenge was held in June, 2012, at Fort Benning, GA. The challenge had four independent events: Endurance, Reconnaissance, Detect, and Disrupt. The Endurance Challenge assessed the speed and endurance of mounted, dismounted, and portable unmanned ground vehicles over an improved road. Reconnaissance assessed sensor acuity, platform mobility and spatial accuracy of small robots required to locate objects in a tactical environment. The Detect Challenge assessed robotic ability to locate simulated pressure-actuated, low and non-metallic IED trigger switches buried at hidden locations along a route. Finally, Disrupt Challenge assessed the effectiveness of robotic vehicles to disrupt the operation of IEDs and their triggers buried at various depths along a roadway representative of one in theater. The two-week event drew participation from 26 vendors.

Ultra-Light Reconnaissance Robot Challenge

In 2011, JIEDDO needed a particular class of robot for the war in Afghanistan. It issued a concrete challenge that expressed the soldiers' needs and were drawn from the suite of Response Robot Performance Standards (National Institute of Standards and Technology (NIST), 2011). Six vendors accepted the challenge and at their own expense brought their robots to NIST for assessment. Some robots met the challenges and others displayed large gaps between promised capability and demonstrated performance. JIEDDO then presented the results of the challenges and the concrete characteristics of the robots to field users in Afghanistan and realized that the original request from the field had been overly constrained. JIEDDO realized from the testing that two classes of robots were needed to address two distinct user communities—an important distinction that was not in the original field request. JIEDDO clarified the challenge and issued a new one. Vendors returned to NIST, again at their own expense, for another opportunity to confront the challenges. This challenge allowed JIEDDO to go from the initial request for help to fielded systems in less than a year.

Mine Resistant Ambush Protected (MRAP) Vehicles

MRAP vehicles are a family of armored fighting vehicles originally designed under the guidance of the U.S. Marine Corps to survive attacks and ambushes involving improvised explosive devices (IEDs). On July 31, 2007, the Marine Corps Systems Command launched MRAP II presolicitation, challenging bidders to develop a new vehicle that offered a higher level of protection than the current MRAP vehicles. The U.S. Army Research Laboratory ensured the technologies used in the Frag Kit 6 upgrade project would be available to MRAP II designers. Initial testing at the Aberdeen Proving Grounds disqualified vehicles that did not meet requirements; the design run-off identified two vendors whose vehicles could pass the demonstration test.

Conclusion

Challenge-based acquisition limits the government's risk by requiring the government to express its needs in terms of concrete challenges. This type of acquisition encourages new players to participate and creates a level playing field for all involved. It provides a path to obtaining superior solutions to vexing, time-critical problems, and fits into the FAR.

OTHER TRANSACTIONS: FOR SCIENTIFIC RESEARCH, TECHNOLOGY DEVELOPMENT, AND PROTOTYPE PROJECTS

Overview

Legal authority for "other transactions" (OT's) differs from agency to agency. The National Aeronautics and Space Administration (NASA) pioneered use of other transactions (Space Act Agreements). Several agencies have authority modeled on authorities granted to the Department of Defense and pioneered at the Defense Advanced Research Projects Agency (DARPA). Other agencies may utilize authorities that are unique to them. The common attribute of Other Transactions is that they are encumbered by fewer procedural rules. Thus setting and accomplishing goals driven by agency mission imperatives rather than compliance with procedural prescriptions is the hallmark of successful OT contracting. The inherent flexibility of OT's, and their attractiveness to a variety of performers, makes OT's well suited for undertaking science, technology, and prototype projects and to engage both traditional and non- traditional performers, as well as consortia and collaborations of academia, commercial firms, and various government agencies.

Conditions for Use of OT's

Some OT statutes require a determination that a standard procurement contract or grant is not feasible or appropriate. Since the Federal Acquisition Regulation (FAR) governs procurement contracts whose principal purpose is the acquisition of goods and services (FAR 35.003) and R&D contracts are stated to be *unlike* contracts for supplies and services (FAR 35.002), that proviso is essentially not a barrier to use of OT's for R&D. Standard assistance instruments (grants) under OMB Circulars are typically awarded to single academic institutions or non-profit research organizations. Research OT's may be awarded to profit-making companies and to consortia including one or more profit-making companies (as well as academic institutions and non-profits).

In other cases, such as DoD's authority to execute prototype projects relevant to weapons systems, OT's may be used even if a procurement contract would be appropriate for the same purpose. Since agency practices such as award of assistance instruments to for-profit firms, contract payments by milestone billings, and other approaches pioneered by OT's have been grafted into the procurement and assistance systems as now in use, it is necessary to consider circumstances as they existed at the time of enactment of the relevant statutes to gain a correct understanding of language such as that relating to *feasibility* or *standard* approaches. Statutory OT language varies and in some cases OT's are simply authorized to carry out agency mission objectives along with other contractual instruments.

Varieties of OT's

There is no existing list of all the variations OT's can take, since due to the flexibility of OT's, all their potential uses and structures have yet to be invented. Several of the innovative contracting techniques described in the other chapters of this document can be adapted for implementation via an "other transaction" agreement. Briefly stated, OT's can take forms that are essentially similar to familiar contracting forms or can look quite different. Many OT's involve a single awardee with other participants being sub-contractors. However, OT's have also involved multiple signatories to the agreement where participant roles are spelled out in the agreement and all participants are in privity of contract with the government. In addition there may be multiple government agencies as parties to the agreement.

Terms and conditions of OT's can differ substantially from typical government contracts or grants. Provisions for intellectual property, changes, dispute resolution, management of the project, termination, and many other matters which are typically imposed by statute or regulation in procurement contracts are subject to negotiation. Thus OT's can take forms that look more like commercial agreements than government contracts.

NASA has entered into a variety of OT's. One of its first was the launch of the first active communications satellite Telstar I (which was funded, developed and owned by AT&T) on a NASA space launch vehicle pursuant to a reimbursable Space Act agreement. More recently, NASA has funded SpaceX to conduct resupply missions to the International Space Station on what are essentially commercial terms and conditions.

DARPA has entered into a variety of OT's including many cost-shared science and technology consortia, notably under the auspices of the Technology Reinvestment Project and other dual-use programs. It has also conducted prototype projects using OT's. Many prototype projects were conducted under the Commercial Operations and Support Savings Initiative while other projects developed full-up military capabilities such as the Global Hawk high endurance unmanned aerial reconnaissance system.

OT's have been used by other agencies in a variety of ways. Some agencies have used OT's to explore new ways of doing business while others have used them in a narrowly tailored fashion, for example, such as only taking advantage of their flexibility in intellectual property.

See the Examples section below for additional variations and characteristics of some OT projects.

Outreach and Solicitation

Competition is the generally preferred but not mandated approach to seeking and evaluating potential projects for award of an OT agreement. The mode of outreach may be essentially similar to that used for the award of standard procurement and assistance instruments or entirely different. If it is important to seek non-traditional performers, then typical government outreach mechanisms and media may be inadequate. Solicitation may be as simple as adding a statement to an open, annual, or project Broad Agency Announcement (BAA) that award instruments may include OT's. This approach, while simple for agency contracting personnel, fails to take full advantage of the flexibility and potential of OT's and does little to address the limits of standard government outreach approaches.

A variation of the basic BAA technique is to use the BAA but allow submission of proposals for award of an OT only and exempt such proposals from data submissions required solely to comply with procedural requirements of the procurement or assistance systems. Another technique is to issue a solicitation similar to a BAA (e.g., "research announcement") but specific to award of OT's and unencumbered by extraneous procedural requirements. Such solicitations should be advertised in media and forums relevant to the technology or business of interest. Solicitations may request not only innovative technical ideas, but also new management and business approaches to accomplishing the underlying objectives of the program.

Entirely different approaches to outreach may be used. This includes employing technology scouts to engage in a worldwide search for relevant innovation and encouraging the submission of what are essentially unsolicited proposals. Scouting may be conducted in person, electronically or preferably in combination. An internet web portal can be used to direct interested parties to the agency technologist who can comment on the relevance of their idea. This process may be considered a form of competition.

Evaluation, Selection, and Award of Proposals

A suitable evaluation process considering the technology stage, likely complexity of the effort, and numbers and types of performers likely to submit proposals should be formulated and outlined in the solicitation or otherwise communicated to prospective offerors prior to the call for proposals. A variety of methods may be employed. For example, white papers/abstracts may precede full proposals with a variety of interactions after submission of abstracts: discussions, up selects (full proposals encouraged) only, up selects and down selects, and so forth. For complex projects, initial selection may be made based on a proposal outline or scoping of the project with detailed proposals submitted phase by phase. Selection may range from the decision of a single scientific officer or group of qualified agency officials, to peer review, to a more elaborate process with multiple panels and levels of review. Peer review is highly valued in some agencies for its openness, the collective expertise it brings to bear, and the venerability and general acceptance of the approach. However, in efforts seeking profound innovation or leaps forward, the possibility of peer review to favor incremental improvement or least common denominator solutions should be considered. The selection official should be a person with expertise and responsibility in the program area or technology involved.

Selection for award may be made after a common cut-off date or in increments if multiple awards are to be made. A public announcement of award should generally be made. If incremental awards are made, announcements may be made award by award or upon the last award. Agencies should state, in the solicitation or otherwise, the manner in which disappointed offerors may submit objections to awards (or failure to receive an award). The procurement protest system under the Government Accountability Office is generally not applicable to the award of OT's; however, objections may always be raised in court and agencies should utilize an administrative process to review and resolve objections before they go to court.

Managing Projects

OT flexibility can be a benefit in managing projects. In complex consortia projects industry participants should be challenged to create governance structures that contribute substantially to project management. As an example, in the Integrated High Performance Turbine Engine Technology (IHPTET) consortium, which included all domestic producers of gas-turbine engines, industry co-funded development of projects related to high performance ceramic components with the government (DARPA, Air Force, NASA). Selection, award, and management of individual projects were vested in the hands of industry participants, with the government setting overall goals for the program. Selection and funding amounts of projects was determined by industry collectively. The uses individual companies made of outcomes remained proprietary.

An important management technique used in many research OT projects is to connect payments to observable technical achievements through milestone billings. Early milestones might be soft so as to infuse start up cash into the project but most milestones should be crafted with considerable rigor. Estimated cost and technical achievement need only be roughly correlated, but the technical milestone needs to be sufficiently relevant that it draws attention to the viability of the planned research approach. Basically milestones should force management assessments of (1) on course, (2) necessity for project termination, or (3) minor or major project realignment needed.

The foregoing paragraphs merely discuss approaches which may make sense for a given project. Traditional project management techniques can be adapted to and used to manage OT's; but when it makes sense, entirely new approaches can be tried. Once an innovative vision for the goals or management of the project has been laid out, it is important to keep the management team focused so that back sliding to business as usual does not take place. Since typical rules applicable to OT's are relatively few, members of the government management team whose role in traditional contracting is largely rule compliance may need to embrace the concept that achieving project goals and application of business judgment are key attributes needed in OT contracting.

Various Cost Issues

Whether an OT project is intended to be fully funded or cost shared, it is important to avoid the lure of imposing standard government cost principles, accounting standards, and other rigid requirements which are sometimes viewed as safeguards but which may in fact not be cost effective. Former Senator Bingaman once characterized government acquisition as a system that spends millions to save thousands. In the case of traditional contractors it may make sense to utilize their government approved business systems, but participants lacking such systems should not typically be required to go to the expense of creating them. Traditional contractors should also be encouraged to seek more cost effective methods. One technique is to organize the project as an Independent Research and Development (IR&D) project. Appropriated funds going to a project organized as an IR&D effort obviously are not allocated to the contractor's IR&D pool. Funded IR&D is possible because, unlike the rule governing procurement contracts, contract funds and IR&D funds can both be used on the same OT effort. This results in substantial savings to the government even absent cost sharing.

Whether or not required by statute, cost sharing or some other form of resource sharing should be considered for each project with commercial potential. In addition to considering current cost sharing, the equities in any potential return from a successfully commercialized project should be considered. It is most important, however, to utilize cost sharing to incentivize performance and increase commitment to project success; not to impose cost sharing requirements that will make successful accomplishment of project goals more difficult. Adjustment of cost sharing makes the most sense when the statutory baseline will impede rather than incentivize performance.

Milestone billing has already been discussed. In addition to its use as an important management tool, the milestone approach avoids reimbursement simply because costs have been incurred but rather connects payments to observable achievements. Milestone events should be sufficiently granular to allow insight into specific accomplishments but not so numerous as to become an administrative burden. Technical members of the government team should be the primary crafters of milestones on the government side with business/contacting specialists in a supporting role.

Innovative Uses of OTs

While it is important for agencies to study past uses of OT's and garner lessons learned, agencies should also consider pioneering new ground utilizing the flexibility inherent in OT's. For example, when the Office of Science and Technology Policy (OSTP) requested information regarding innovation expediting translational research and time to market in the biotechnology sector, it received a proposal outlining an innovative means for financing government funded research projects that would reduce costs, mitigate "valleys of death," and coordinate various phases of research conducted by different government agencies or bureaus. A multi-party OT agreement was proposed as the glue that brought various moving parts of a new financing system together.

Case Studies of Selected OTs

NASA: Joint Endeavor Agreements

The Joint Endeavor Agreement (JEA) was a class of OT's utilized by NASA to encourage private investment in research to be conducted aboard the Space Shuttle. In a JEA NASA provided a flight into space aboard the Shuttle for the private party's experiment which sometimes included a private sector researcher (payload specialist). The private party bore the expense of its research, equipment, and its personnel but did not pay a fee to NASA for transportation to space. This arrangement supported NASA's mission to encourage utilization of space as well as research into space flight. NASA had full visibility into the private sector activity for purposes of safety and compatibility with other experiments, but insight into research results was negotiable up to the point of being fully proprietary.

The earliest use of a JEA was to develop Continuous Flow Electrophoresis. Early experiments were process oriented and sponsored by McDonnell Douglas Astronautics Company. Later the pharmaceutical company Johnson and Johnson conducted electrophoresis in space in order to separate substances difficult to isolate in Earth's 1-g environment. Still later other companies entered into JEA's to isolate or purify a variety of organic and inorganic materials aboard the Shuttle including, for example, 3M Corporation.

The first JEA was conducted on the fourth Space Shuttle flight and a large variety of successful experiments addressing a wide range of technologies were flown during the course of the Shuttle program.

DARPA: Joint Unmanned Combat Air Systems (JUCAS)

DARPA, the Air Force, and the Navy combined to develop a system of highly capable unmanned combat air vehicles networked through a common operating system. These vehicles are to penetrate deep into high threat environments, be survivable and constitute a persistent combat capability. The program involved major defense companies, Boeing and Northrop, as well as significant roles for nontraditional contractors. The X-45 and X-47 experimental aircraft resulted from the program.

Cost was reduced in this program because both major contractors organized their efforts as IR&D projects (allowed under OT's; government payments off-set IR&D balances), eliminating general and administrative expenses; facilities capital and cost of money; fee; and reducing labor and material rates by about 15%. In addition Boeing invested about $300 million in the effort. Cost was also saved because the streamlined management and change order processes adopted were estimated to reduce schedule by more than a year.

The flexibility of the OT helped attract nontraditional companies to the project. Some were unique including a supplier of composite materials whose main line of business was manufacturing surfboards. In the case of Northrop Grumman, nontraditional companies provided essential capabilities. The differing nature of the participants and highly innovative nature of the project operating at close to the state of the art resulted in adjustments in industry's position on intellectual property matters. The OT could accommodate flexible IP arrangements.

The project was financed through payable milestones which both improved cash flow and focused the project on key technical accomplishments. Milestone payments incentivized contractors to achieve observable results at less than estimated cost. Milestones were modified in the light of experience. This type of flexibility would have been difficult to achieve under a FAR contract with inflexible contract line item numbers.

NGA: *Chemical, Biological and Radiological Technology Alliance (CBRTA)*

The CBRTA was part of a multifaceted consortium (National Technology Alliance) authorized by Congress to inject commercial technologies for security and defense needs. It consisted of thirteen commercial firms and academic institutions, awarded under an OT agreement, with 3M leading the consortium in an administrative capacity. The National Geospatial-Intelligence Agency (NGA) acted as executive agent and provided the contracting support.

CBRTA afforded the government access to a reservoir of intellectual talent consisting of thousands of the best and brightest scientists and engineers employed by the CBRTA member companies and institutions. Projects were initiated as a modification to the basic agreement in the form of task orders. Because industry could formulate a program plan in response to a government need in a matter of days (potentially hours), work could begin under an approved plan almost as quickly. Work could be performed by members of the Alliance or subcontracted if the requisite expertise existed outside CBRTA companies.

Administrative costs were funded separately from R&D efforts. Most projects were funded as time and materials efforts while others were either cost-reimbursement or fixed price milestones. The government obtained the leverage of industry investment which was often five or ten times that of the government in many of the technologies supported by CBRTA member companies. Project time was shortened due to the reduced need for cost and pricing data, elimination of a formal engineering change process, and simplified terms and conditions with suppliers, all due to the fact that the OT instrument included these terms and conditions.

This type of consortium embraces nontraditional participants both as members of the consortium and also in the subcontract role. OT allows flexibility in intellectual property as well as government-unique requirements such as hourly timecard reporting and DCAA compliance, which could be nonstarters for many of the companies and scientists involved in CBRTA projects.

DOD: *Hummingbird Unmanned Aerial Vehicle*

The A-160 Hummingbird UAV is rotor-craft built by Frontier Systems, a small nontraditional contractor. It incorporated revolutionary rotor technology and is intended for reconnaissance; surveillance; target acquisition; communications relay; and precision resupply missions in autonomous operation. It has long endurance and can fly thousands of feet higher than conventional helicopters. Hummingbird has successfully undergone flight tests and has been used in a number of tests for operational applications.

A section 845 OT proved to be very cost-effective. It enabled dealing with the small commercial firm and particularly held down cost in the early R&D phase. Cost savings additionally accrued through time savings in both the pre- and post-award phases and as a result of the streamlined changes process. This work would likely not have occurred under a FAR-based contract, as Frontier Systems may not have accepted such a contract.

Particularly important in this case was flexibility in intellectual property, especially patent rights, as Frontier has patented inventions related to its revolutionary rotor technology. The flexibility of an OT to accommodate the needs of a performer with specific needs or revolutionary ideas of importance to DOD was demonstrated in this project.

DOD: Dual-Use and Commercial Operations and Support Savings Initiative (COSSI)

While JUCAS and Hummingbird are examples of individual section 845 OT programs, major successes have also been achieved in broad programs involving hundreds of agreements, including DOD's dual-use technology programs (originally the DARPA-led Technology Reinvestment Project) and COSSI. The dual- use programs used the original (10 U.S.C. 2371) OT authority and COSSI were executed using a combination of the original authority and section 845 OT agreements.

DARPA's success in promoting dual-use technologies (those with both commercial and military applications) through cost shared collaborations with commercial firms using OT contracting was such that it led a distinguished panel under retired Marine General Al Gray to recommend the dual-use approach as the DOD's primary means of undertaking new technology developments. Other reports also found that these OT programs were highly successful.

COSSI was a program started in 1997 that aimed to reduce operations and support costs by replacing (often expensive and outdated) military specific components in DOD systems with components adapted from commercial products or technology. The program was premised on DOD funding the modification, testing, and adaptation of the commercial component for military needs on a cost shared basis while the commercial partner gained the promise of a fixed price procurement if the savings was successfully demonstrated. Since OT production authority did not exist, COSSI was designed to use FAR Part 12 commercial item contracts for the follow-on procurement. COSSI was successful in the sense that documented OS cost savings exceeding the government's R&D investment were realized, and eventually the program attracted considerable participation by nontraditional firms.

In both the dual-use programs and COSSI, flexibility in intellectual property rights and streamlined business practices were important to attracting commercial firms. These programs were competitive in nature, but the competitions held were more informal than competitions under Part 15 of the FAR and generally resembled the broad agency announcements.

DHS: BioAgent Autonomous Network Detector (BAND) Program

The purpose of the BAND Program is to develop a detect-to-treat biological detection sensor system that provides more rapid indications of the presence of biological agents compared to current state-of- the-art technology. This program developed the next generation of BioWatch detectors and is critical to the BioWatch program. Currently, the BioWatch system consists of distributed collectors that sample on filters that are collected and centrally processed at local laboratories, which has not provided information in as timely a response as DHS would have liked.

With the use of OT Authority, DHS was able to prototype and test three BAND systems from three firms: IQuum, Microfluidic Systems, and U.S. Genomics. While each system is different, the systems have performed up to the rigorous objectives set by DHS. DHS objectives include having: a very high sensitivity in a cluttered background; an extended coverage area, i.e., with a networked system as opposed to a manual collection system; a very low false alarm rate, range of 1 per 10 to 100 years; and a low cost of ownership. Due to the projected reduced costs of these systems, a larger portion of the Nation's population will be protected without incurring additional costs and with equivalent or better performance.

The BAND Program resulted from Broad Agency Announcement (BAA) designed to obtain proposals from teams that cut across organizational boundaries to achieve optimal mixes of talent and innovation. The BAA specified that DHS would use its OT Authority to attract traditional and non-traditional firms individually and as teams.

End Notes

[1] http://dupress.com/articles/the-craft-of-incentive-prize-design/

[2] http://mckinseyonsociety.com/capturing-the-promise-of-philanthropic-prizes/

[3] http://dash.harvard.edu/bitstream/handle/1/3351241/Jeppesen_Marginality.pdf?sequence=2

[4] http://www.whitehouse.gov/sites/default/files/omb/assets/memoranda_2010/m10-11.pdf

[5] http://www.challenge.gov/

[6] http://www.gpo.gov/fdsys/pkg/BILLS-111hr5116enr/pdf/BILLS-111hr5116enr.pdf

[7] http://dash.harvard.edu/bitstream/handle/1/3351241/Jeppesen_Marginality.pdf?sequence=2

[8] http://www.mckinseyonsociety.com/downloads/reports/Social-Innovation/And_the_winner_ is. pdf

[9] http://dupress.com/articles/the-craft-of-incentive-prize-design/

[10] http://www.gavialliance.org/funding/pneumococcal-amc/about/

[11] http://energy.gov/articles/federal-and-industry-partners-issue-challenge-manufacturers

[12] http://www4.eere.energy.gov/alliance/activities/technology-solutions-teams/space-conditioning/rtu

[13] http://mainecite.org/index.php/education/2-uncategorised/21-cooperative-buying-consortium-for-schools

[14] http://www.whitehouse.gov/omb/factsheet/paying-for-success

[15] http://www.nyc.gov/portal/site/nycgov/menuitem.c0935b9a57bb4ef3daf2f1c701c789a0/ index.jsp?pageID=mayor_press_release&catID=1194&doc_name=http%3A%2F%2Fwww. nyc.gov%2Fhtml%2Fom%2Fhtml%2F2012b%2Fpr285-12.html&cc=unused1978&rc= 1194&ndi=1http://www.nytimes.com/2012/08/02/nyregion/goldman-to-invest-   in-new-york-city-jail-program.html

[16] http://www.nasa.gov/offices/c3po/about/c3po.html

[17]   http://www.fda.gov/AboutFDA/CentersOffices/OfficeofMedicalProductsandTobacco/CDRH/ CDRHInnovation/Inno vationPathway/default.htm

[18] http://www.uspto.gov/patents/init_events/patents_for_humanity.jsp

[19] http://www.nber.org/papers/w6304

[20] http://cyber.law.harvard.edu/publications/2012/public_private_partnerships_for_organizing_ and_executing_priz e-based_competitions

[21] http://www.howto.gov/communities/challenges-and-prizes-community

[22] http://www.whitehouse.gov/blog/2012/06/12/unleashing-innovation-deepening-democracy-through-prizes-0

[23] https://cio.gov/wp-content/uploads/downloads/2012/09/Prize_Authority_in_the_America_ COMPETES_Reauthorization_Act.pdf

[24] http://www.whitehouse.gov/sites/default/files/omb/assets/memoranda_2010/m10-11.pdf

[25] http://www.hhs.gov/open/initiatives/challenges

[26]   http://www.howto.gov/sites/default/files/competitions-challenges-services-fas.pptx (PowerPoint presentation)

[27] http://www.nasa.gov/offices/COECI/index.html

[28] http://dupress.com/articles/the-craft-of-incentive-prize-design/

[29] More information on eligibility and judging requirements under America COMPETES can be found here: https://cio.gov/wp- content/uploads/downloads/2012/09/Prize_Authority_ in_the_America_COMPETES_Reauthorization_Act.pdf

[30] http://www.innocentive.com/

[31] http://www.topcoder.com/

[32] http://www.gsaelibrary.gsa.gov/ElibMain/sinDetails.do?scheduleNumber=541&special ItemNumber=541+4G&exec uteQuery=YES

[33] http://flagsuit.com/

[34] http://www.iprizecleanoceans.org/teams/elastec

[35] http://www.nasa.gov/pdf/572344main_InnoCentive_NASA_PublicReport_2011-0422.pdf

[36] http://www.whitehouse.gov/blog/2011/06/27/competition-shines-light-dark-matter

[37] http://host.kaggle.com/casestudies/mdm

[38] http://archive.darpa.mil/grandchallenge/

[39] http://challenge.gov/ONC/208-using-public-data-for-cancer-prevention-and-control-from-innovation -to-impact

[40] http://www.mycancergenome.org/

[41] http://www.mc.vanderbilt.edu/reporter/index.html?ID=12436

[42] http://axialexchange.com/

[43] http://cts.businesswire.com/ct/CT?id=smartlink&div=bfhbgigcig&url=http%3A%2F%2F www.health2news.com%2F2011%2F12%2F14%2Fcongratulations-to-the-winners-of-the-ensuring-safe-transitions-innovation-challenge%2F&esheet=50310850&lan=en-   US& anchor=Ensuring+Safe+Transitions+From+Hospital+to+Home&index=8&md5=f74410563 23d105fc2e7dd04ccf a6de7

[44] http://mckinseyonsociety.com/capturing-the-promise-of-philanthropic-prizes

[45] Office of Management and Budget memorandum M-10-11, "Guidance on the Use of Challenges and Prizes to Promote OpenGovernment"; http://www.whitehouse.gov/sites/ default/files/omb/assets/memoranda_2010/m10-11.pdf

[46] Challenge-Based Acquisition Handbook, 2nd edition, MITRE Corporation: www.mitre.org/ publications/technical- papers/challenge-based-acquisition-2nd-edition

[47] "Challenge-Based Acquisition: Stimulating Innovative Solutions Faster and Cheaper by Asking the Right Questions" www.acquisitionresearch.net/files/FY2013/NPS-AM-13-C10P01R013 -042.pdf

[48] FAR 1.102-4: Role of the Acquisition Team.

In: Innovative Federal Contracting: Case Studies   ISBN: 978-1-63463-440-3
Editor: Darrel Cobb   © 2015 Nova Science Publishers, Inc.

Chapter 2

COMPETITION IN FEDERAL CONTRACTING: A LEGAL OVERVIEW*

Kate M. Manuel

SUMMARY

Competition in federal procurement contracting has long been of interest to Congress and the executive branch, in part because of the belief that increased competition among potential vendors results in lower prices for the government. President Obama issued a memorandum calling for increased competition in federal contracting on March 4, 2009, shortly after taking office, and his Administration has sought to reduce the number of "noncompetitive" contracts by various means, including by issuing guidance on "Increasing Competition and Structuring Contracts for Best Results" in October 2009. Most recently, the Department of Defense (DOD), which generally accounts for nearly 70% of federal procurement spending per year, began implementing regulations that would promote competition by generally requiring contracting officers to re-solicit agency requirements if a solicitation allowed fewer than 30 days for the receipt of proposals and resulted in only one bid or offer.

The Competition in Contracting Act (CICA) of 1984 generally governs competition in federal procurement contracting. Any procurement contract not entered into through the use of procurement

---

* This is an edited, reformatted and augmented version of a Congressional Research Service publication R40516, prepared for Members and Committees of Congress, dated January 11, 2013.

procedures expressly authorized by a particular statute is subject to CICA. CICA requires that contracts be entered into after "full and open competition through the use of competitive procedures" unless certain circumstances exist that would permit agencies to use noncompetitive procedures. Full and open competition can be obtained through the use of sealed bids, competitive proposals, or other procures defined as competitive under CICA (e.g., procurement of architectural or engineering services under the Brooks Act). Full and open competition under CICA also encompasses "full and open competition after exclusion of sources," such as results when agencies engage in dual sourcing or set aside acquisitions for small businesses.

Any contract entered into without full and open competition is noncompetitive, but noncompetitive contracts can still be in compliance with CICA when circumstances permitting other than full and open competition exist. CICA recognizes seven such circumstances, including (1) single source for goods or services; (2) unusual and compelling urgency; (3) maintenance of the industrial base; (4) requirements of international agreements; (5) statutory authorization or acquisition of brand-name items for resale; (6) national security; and (7) contracts necessary in the public interest. CICA also allows agencies to use "special simplified procedures" when acquiring goods or services whose expected value is less than $150,000, or commercial goods or services whose expected value is less than $6.5 million ($12 million in emergencies).

Issuance of orders under task order and delivery order (TO/DO) contracts is not subject to CICA, although award of TO/DO contracts is. However, the Federal Acquisition Streamlining Act (FASA) of 1994 established a preference for multiple-award TO/DO contracts; required that agencies provide contractors "a fair opportunity" to compete for orders in excess of $3,000 under multiple-award contracts; and authorized the Government Accountability Office (GAO) to hear protests challenging the issuance of task or delivery orders that increase the scope, period, or maximum value of the underlying contract. The National Defense Authorization Act (NDAA) for FY2008 further limited the use of single-award TO/DO contracts. It also specified what constitutes a "fair opportunity to be considered" for orders in excess of $5.5 million under multiple-award contracts and granted GAO exclusive jurisdiction to hear protests of orders valued in excess of $10 million that do not increase the scope, period, or maximum value of the contract. This jurisdiction is permanent as to protests of defense agency contracts (P.L. 112-239), but only lasts through September 30, 2016, for protests of civilian agency contracts (P.L. 112-81).

INTRODUCTION

"Procurement" describes the process whereby the government obtains goods and services from private parties that it does not produce or provide for itself. Competition in government procurement means that the government determines from whom to buy goods and services—and thus with whom to contract—by "solicit[ing] or entertain[ing] offers from two or more competitors, compar[ing] them, and accept[ing] one based on its relative value."[1]

Competition in federal procurement contracting has long been of interest to Congress and the executive branch, in part because of the belief that increased competition among potential vendors results in lower prices for the government.[2] President Obama issued a memorandum calling for increased competition in federal contracting on March 4, 2009, shortly after taking office,[3] and his Administration has sought to reduce the number of "noncompetitive" contracts by various means, including by issuing guidance on "Increasing Competition and Structuring Contracts for Best Results" in October 2009.[4] Most recently, the Department of Defense (DOD), which generally accounts for nearly 70% of federal procurement spending per year,[5] began implementing regulations that would promote competition by generally requiring contracting officers to re-solicit agency requirements if a solicitation allowed fewer than 30 days for the receipt of proposals and resulted in only one bid or offer.[6]

Recent Congresses have also sought to promote competition in federal contracting by enacting legislation that

- limits the use of appropriated funds to procure certain items until the procuring agency certifies to Congress that its acquisition strategy meets certain requirements pertaining to competition;[7]
- requires agencies to establish goals for competition for certain contracts,[8] processes for measuring competition for certain contracts,[9] and/or annual reviews of certain contracts;[10]
- precludes defense agencies from awarding noncompetitive contracts based on unsolicited research proposals;[11]
- requires DOD to take further steps to foster competition in the procurement of "major defense acquisition programs";[12] and
- requires that certain recipients of federal grants or financial assistance obtain competition when awarding contracts.[13]

This report describes the competition requirements currently governing the procurement activities of federal agencies. It addresses (1) what contracts are subject to competition requirements; (2) what constitutes full and open competition for government contracts; (3) what is meant by "full and open competition after exclusion of sources"; (4) the circumstances permitting agencies to award contracts on the basis of other than full and open competition; (5) the "special simplified procedures for small purchases"; and (6) the competition requirements for task order and delivery order (TO/DO) contracts. The report does not address so-called "public-private competitions" or "competitive sourcing targets" under the Federal Activities Inventory Reform (FAIR) Act or Office of Management and Budget (OMB) Circular A-76.[14] Public-private competitions are conducted to determine whether government employees or private contractors will perform functions formerly performed by the government that have been identified as commercial and suitable for contracting out.[15]

BACKGROUND

The federal government has promoted competition between offerors seeking to meet its needs since at least 1781, when the Superintendent of Finance advertised in a local newspaper for proposals from potential suppliers of food for federal employees in Philadelphia.[16] Then, as now, the government encouraged competition because of its reported benefits to the government and the general public. Proponents of competition note that when multiple offerors compete for the government's business, the government can acquire higher quality goods and services at lower prices than it would acquire if it awarded contracts without competition. Proponents also note that competition helps to curb fraud because it allows for periodic changes in the vendors from which the government acquires goods and services, thereby limiting opportunities for government employees to enter into collusive agreements with their regular suppliers. Competition is similarly said to promote accountability by ensuring that contracts are entered into on their merits and not upon any other basis (e.g., familial or other relationships between contracting officers and contractors). Further, because the government is said to acquire the highest quality goods and services at the lowest prices, proponents of competition note that competition helps government officials reassure citizens that their tax dollars are not spent wastefully. Finally, proponents of competition claim that citizens are less likely to perceive contracts as being awarded because of favoritism when there is competition.

Competition is not considered an unmitigated good by all, however, as is noted by those who advocate for certain limits on competition. Such commentators have pointed out that agency operations can be delayed by the time it takes to solicit and evaluate offers from eligible suppliers. These delays are reportedly especially harmful when agencies are contracting for goods or services for disaster responses or military operations. Moreover, because there are costs involved in agencies' soliciting and evaluating offers, these commentators note that there comes a point when the government's costs in competing contracts are greater than the savings it realizes from the lower price, higher quality goods it obtains through competition. It was, in part, for this reason that the drafters of the Competition in Contracting Act (CICA) of 1984[17] opted to require full and open competition rather than maximum competition. They reportedly considered language calling for "maximum competition,"[18] but rejected it, in part, because "there is a point of diminishing return" with competition.[19] Proponents of limits on competition further note that competition can increase the risk that government contractors will be unable to perform by allowing new contractors—who do not have experience meeting agencies' needs or complying with the accounting and paperwork requirements imposed on federal contractors—to win government contracts. Agencies reportedly would prefer to deal with their incumbent contractors, assuming these contractors are competent, because they represent "known quantities" for the agencies.[20]

As the accompanying chronology illustrates, the federal government's requirements for competition in contracting have periodically shifted as the government has variously sought to realize the benefits of competition or further other goals, such as the protection of national security in times of war or efficiency in agency operations, in its procurement activities. Armed conflicts, in particular, typically lead to relaxation of competition requirements, but often result in alleged abuses—such as "war profiteering" by contractors and waste of money on overpriced goods and services—that later lead to increased competition requirements.[21]

Chronology

1809	Congress passes the first law requiring competition in federal procurement contracting. This law established what came to be known as "formal advertising" as the preferred method for federal procurements by specifying that "all purchases and contracts for supplies or services ... shall be made by open purchases, or by previously advertising for proposals." (2 Stat. 536 (1809)).
1861	Congress reaffirms its commitment to formal advertising by passing a statute stating that "all purchases and contracts for supplies and services, ... except for personal services, ... shall be made by advertising a sufficient time previously for proposals respecting the same" unless immediate delivery is required due to "public exigencies." (12 Stat. 220 (1861)).
1914-1918	The War Industries Board authorizes negotiated procurements, or procurements involving bargaining with the offerors after receipt of proposals. Such procurements are classified as noncompetitive.
1930	The War Policies Commission recommends that formal advertising be replaced by negotiated procurement during times of war. Congress does not enact this proposed change, but does recognize additional exceptions allowing use of negotiated procurement instead of formal advertising.
1939-1945	In December 1941, Congress passes the First War Powers Act, which authorizes the President to grant agencies that are "involved in the war" authority to enter into contracts "without regard to the provision of law relating to the making, performance, amendment, or modifications of contracts." (55 Stat. 838 (1941)). Later in the war, the War Production Board prohibits agencies from using formal advertising without specific authorization to do so.
1945	A task force of the Procurement Policy Board, consisting of officers from the federal procuring agencies, recommends relaxing competition requirements to support the growth and sustainability of the industrial base.
1947	Congress passes the Armed Services Procurement Act (ASPA), which generally requires use of formal advertising but allows use of negotiated procurements when any of 17 exceptions apply. These exceptions address things such as medicines or medical property; property purchased for authorized resale; perishable or nonperishable subsistence supplies; and property or services for which it is impracticable to secure competition. ASPA only applies to the procurement contracts of defense agencies.
1949	Congress passes the Federal Property and Administrative Services Act (FPASA), subjecting civilian agencies to requirements like those in ASPA. FPASA recognizes 15 exceptions to formal advertising.
1982	Senators William V. Roth, Jr., Carl Levin, and William S. Cohen first introduce the Competition in Contracting Act (CICA) (S. 2127). Increased competition in contracting is also among the "Carlucci Initiatives," 32 steps for reforming defense acquisitions announced by then Deputy Secretary of Defense Frank Carlucci.

1984	Congress passes CICA, requiring agencies to obtain "full and open competition through the use of competitive procedures" in their procurement activities unless otherwise authorized by law.
1990-1991	Military agencies reportedly experience difficulties in procuring commercial items for use during the Gulf War.
1994	Congress passes the Federal Acquisition Streamlining Act (FASA), which establishes a "preference" for the acquisition of commercial items in meeting agencies' procurement needs. FASA also articulates competition requirements for task order and delivery order (TO/DO) contracts.
1996	Congress passes the Federal Acquisition Reform Act (FARA), which requires that agencies "obtain full and open competition ... in a manner that is consistent with the need to efficiently fulfill the Government's requirements." FARA also relaxes the rules imposed on agencies' purchases of commercial items.
2003	Congress passes the Services Acquisition Reform Act (SARA). SARA further relaxes the rules imposed upon procurement of commercial services.
2008	Section 843 of the National Defense Authorization Act for FY2008 limits the use of single-award task order/delivery order (TO/DO) contracts in excess of $100 million; grants GAO temporary jurisdiction over protests involving orders of $10 million or more; and specifies what constitutes a "fair opportunity to be considered" for orders in excess of $5 million.[22]

The current interest in competition in contracting is perhaps to be expected given developments in the 25 years since the enactment of CICA. CICA itself requires that agencies "obtain full and open competition through the use of competitive procedures" in all procurements not involving the use of procedures expressly authorized by a particular statute.[23] CICA remains the foundation for the current competition requirements, but has been amended or supplemented by later laws that place efficiency in agency operations or other public benefits on par with competition, or expand agencies' ability to use "special simplified methods" for contracting for commercial items. The Federal Acquisition Streamlining Act (FASA) of 1994, for example, establishes a "preference" for the procurement of commercial items, which generally may be acquired using simplified methods, as opposed to full and open competition.[24] FASA was followed by the Federal Acquisition Reform Act (FARA) of 1996, which placed increasing emphasis on efficiency in agency operations by requiring that the Federal Acquisition Regulation (FAR) be amended to "ensure that the requirement to obtain full and open competition is implemented in a manner that is consistent with the need to efficiently fulfill the Government's requirements."[25] FARA and the Services Acquisition Reform Act (SARA) of 2003[26] also relaxed the rules governing agencies' acquisition of commercial items. More recently, the Emergency

Economic Stabilization Act (EESA) of 2008 authorized the Secretary of the Treasury to use other than full and open competition upon determining "that urgent and compelling circumstances make compliance with [the competition] provisions contrary to the public interest."[27] This provision was designed to ensure that competition requirements, among other things, did not slow the Treasury Department's contracting for services that would help stabilize U.S. financial markets and the banking system.[28]

CONTRACTS NOT SUBJECT TO CICA

Not all contracts—or even all procurement contracts—that agencies lawfully enter into are the result of full and open competition under CICA or an "exception" to it.[29] Non-procurement contracts, such as those resulting from agencies' use of other transaction authority (OTA) or similar authorities, are not subject to CICA because they are not procurement contracts, and CICA only applies to "procurement procedures."[30] OTA refers to agencies' authority to enter into an "other transaction," or "a form of contract ... that is not a procurement contract, grant, or cooperative agreement."[31] Only a few agencies, most notably the Departments of Defense, Transportation, Homeland Security, Health and Human Services, and Energy, at various times, have been granted OTA so that they can contract for research and development (R&D) or prototypes of promising new technologies without full and open competition.[32] Contracting for R&D or prototypes can be difficult because the uncertainties inherent in the development of new technologies make it hard to establish contract prices. Additionally, the companies best able to perform such contracts are often not regular government vendors and may be unwilling or unable to comply with the government's procurement regulations. OTA helps to avoid these difficulties.

Also not subject to the requirement for full and open competition under CICA are those procurement contracts entered into through the "use of procurement procedures ... expressly authorized by statute."[33] There are numerous statutory provisions that allow agencies to use specific procurement procedures in certain circumstances, or otherwise allow them to limit competition for procurement contracts. One provision of the Consolidated Appropriations Act for FY2005, for example, allowed the U.S. Agency for International Development to place task orders with small or small disadvantaged businesses in lieu of providing a "fair opportunity" for all eligible firms to compete.[34] Other provisions of this law allowed agencies to limit competition to certain groups or entities, notwithstanding CICA, or to enter into contracts without competition.[35]

CONTRACTS SUBJECT TO CICA

Any procurement contract not entered into through the use of procedures expressly authorized by a particular statute, such as those described above, is subject to CICA.[36] CICA requires that these contracts be entered into after "full and open competition through the use of competitive procedures" unless certain circumstances exist that would permit agencies to use noncompetitive procedures.[37]

Full and Open Competition Defined

Under CICA, "full and open competition" results when "all responsible sources are permitted to submit sealed bids or competitive proposals."[38] A responsible source is a prospective contractor who (1) has adequate financial resources to perform the contract, or the ability to acquire such resources; (2) is able to comply with the required or proposed delivery or performance schedule; (3) has a satisfactory performance record; (4) has a satisfactory record of integrity and business ethics; (5) has the necessary organization, experience, technical skills, and accounting and operational controls, or the ability to obtain them; (6) has the necessary production, construction, and technical equipment and facilities, or the ability to obtain them; and (7) is otherwise qualified and eligible to receive an award under applicable laws and regulations.[39]

Competitive Procedures Resulting in Full and Open Competition

Agencies meet CICA's requirement for full and open competition by using one of the "competitive procedures" recognized under the act.[40] CICA recognizes the following procedures as competitive:

1. *Sealed bids.* Sealed bids are offers submitted in response to invitations for bids (IFBs); opened publicly at a specified time and place; and evaluated without discussions with the bidders, with the contract

being awarded to the lowest-priced responsible bidder.[41] CICA requires that agencies solicit sealed bids if (1) time permits their solicitation, submission, and evaluation; (2) the award will be made on the basis of price and other price-related factors; (3) it is not necessary to conduct discussions with bidders about their bids; and (4) there is a reasonable expectation of receiving more than one sealed bid.[42]

2. *Competitive Proposals.* Agencies are to use competitive proposals whenever "sealed bids are not appropriate" in light of the previous four factors.[43]

3. Competitive proposals are offers received in response to requests for proposals (RFPs). RFPs generally provide for discussion or negotiation between the government and at least those offerors within the "competitive range," with the contract being awarded to the responsible offeror whose proposal represents the "best value" for the government.[44]

4. *Combinations of competitive procedures.* These include procedures like two-step sealed bidding. With two-step sealed bidding, the first step consists of the submission, evaluation and, potentially, discussion of technical proposals from each bidder with no pricing involved. In the second step, sealed bids are submitted only by those who submitted technically acceptable proposals during the first step.

5. *Procurement of architectural or engineering services* conducted in accordance with the requirements of the Brooks Act (40 U.S.C. §§541-559). The Brooks Act allows the selection of architects and engineers based upon their qualifications without consideration of the proposed price for the work. Awards must be made to the highest-ranked offeror unless a reasonable price cannot be agreed upon.

6. *Competitive selection of basic research proposals* resulting from a general solicitation and peer or scientific review of proposals, or from a solicitation conducted pursuant to 15 U.S.C. Section 638 (research and development contracts for small businesses).

7. *Procedures established by the General Services Administration (GSA) for its multiple awards schedule program.* Such procedures are recognized as competitive so long as participation in the GSA program is open to all responsible sources, and orders and contracts under GSA's procedures result in the lowest overall cost alternative to meet the government's needs.

8. *Procurements conducted in pursuant to 15 U.S.C. Section 644.* Section 644 addresses set-asides for small businesses, among other things. Such set-asides are competitive so long as all responsible businesses entitled to submit offers under Section 644 are permitted to compete.[45]

The sixth of these provisions is particularly significant because it allows agencies to use the so-called "Federal Supply Schedules" (FSS) or "GSA schedules." These schedules enable agencies to take advantage of a "simplified process" for obtaining commercial supplies and services by issuing task or delivery orders directly to contractors listed on the schedules without issuing IFBs or RFPs.[46] The seventh provision is also significant because it authorizes "set-asides" for small businesses, which constitute "full and open competition after exclusion of sources" and are discussed below.[47]

"Full and Open Competition After Exclusion of Sources"

Some competitions in which only certain contractors can compete nonetheless meet CICA's requirement for full and open competition because CICA provides for "full and open competition after exclusion of sources."[48] "Full and open competition after exclusion of sources" occurs in two contexts: agencies' "dual sourcing" initiatives and set-asides for small businesses.[49]

The defense agencies, in particular, have a lengthy history of dual sourcing, or distributing their contracts for particular goods or services among multiple manufacturers or suppliers in order to ensure that their operations are not vulnerable to the fortunes of individual companies.[50] CICA recognizes this history, and the agency concerns underlying it, by stating that agencies:

> may provide for the procurement of property or services covered by this section using competitive procedures but excluding a particular source in order to establish or maintain any alternative source or sources of supply for that property or service if the agency head determines that to do so—
>
> a)   would increase or maintain competition and would likely result in reduced overall costs for such procurement, or for any anticipated procurement, of such property and services;
>
> b)   would be in the interest of national defense in having a facility (or a producer, manufacturer, or other supplier) available for furnishing the property or service in the case of a national emergency or industrial mobilization;

  c)   would be in the interest of national defense in establishing or
       maintaining an essential engineering, research, or development
       capability to be provided by an educational or other nonprofit
       institution or a federally funded research and development center;
  d)   would ensure the continuous availability of a reliable source of
       supply of such property or service;
  e)   would satisfy projected needs for such property or service
       determined on the basis of a history of high demand for the
       property or service; or
  f)   in the case of medical supplies, safety supplies, or emergency
       supplies, would satisfy a critical need for such supplies.[51]

Recently, Congress has sometimes mandated dual sourcing, especially by
the Department of Defense (DOD), in order to ensure competition in future
procurements.[52]

CICA similarly recognizes the history of setting aside acquisitions for
competitions limited to small businesses in general, or to specific subcategories
of small businesses, by allowing "procurement of property or services ... using
competitive procedures, but excluding other than small business concerns."[53]
The Small Business Act provides for such set-asides for small businesses
generally; women-owned, service-disabled veteran-owned and Historically
Underutilized Business Zone (HUBZone) small businesses; and small
businesses owned and controlled by socially and economically disadvantaged
individuals that are participating in the Business Development Program under
Section 8(a) of the act.[54] Set-asides can also be made for local firms during
major disasters or emergencies under the authority of the Stafford Act (42
U.S.C. §5150).[55]

Circumstances Permitting Other Than Full and Open Competition

By definition, under CICA, any procurement contract entered into without
full and open competition is noncompetitive.[56] This is not to say, however, that
every procurement contract entered into without using competitive procedures
is in violation of CICA. This is because CICA recognizes seven circumstances
wherein agencies can use other than competitive procedures without violating
the act's competition requirements.[57] Such circumstances involve the
following:

1) *Single source for goods or services*: The property or services needed by the agency are available from only one responsible source and no other type of property or service satisfies the agency's needs.

2) *Unusual and compelling circumstances*: The agency's need for property or services is of such an unusual and compelling urgency that the government would be seriously injured unless the agency is permitted to limit the number of sources from which it solicits bids or proposals.[58]

3) *Maintenance of the industrial base*: It is necessary to award the contract to a particular source or sources in order (1) to maintain a facility, producer, manufacturer, or other supplier so that the maintained entity will be available to furnish property or services in the case of a national emergency or to achieve industrial mobilization; or (2) to establish or maintain an essential engineering, research, or development capability to be provided by an educational or other nonprofit institution or a federally funded research and development center.

4) *Requirements of international agreements*: The terms of an international agreement or treaty between the United States and a foreign government or international organization, or the written directions of a foreign government reimbursing a federal agency for the cost of procuring property or services, effectively require the use of procedures other than competitive procedures.

5) *Statutory authorization or acquisition of brand-name items for resale*: A statute expressly authorizes or requires that the procurement be made through another executive agency or from a specified source, or the agency's need is for brand-name commercial items for authorized resale.

6) *National security*: Disclosure of the agency's procurement needs would compromise national security unless the agency is permitted to limit the number of sources from which it solicits bids or proposals.

7) *Necessary in the public interest*: The head of an executive agency determines that it is necessary in the public interest to use other than competitive procedures in the procurement and notifies Congress in writing of this determination no less than 30 days before the award of the contract.[59]

These "exceptions" cover common situations where competition is not possible, or where the government values other objectives (e.g., maintaining the industrial base) more highly than full and open competition. The first exception, for example, allows what are commonly known as "sole-source awards." By law, sole-source awards can be used only when there is a single responsible source and no other supplies or services will satisfy agency requirements. Although sole-source awards have been the subject of much reported concern recently, especially among those worried about the alleged increase in their use since FY2000,[60] they can help agencies to efficiently meet their needs for goods and services when circumstances suggest there is little or no possibility of competition. The first exception also encompasses agencies' acceptance of unsolicited research proposals, as well as follow-on contracts for continued development or production of major systems.[61] The second exception covers many so-called contingency contracting situations, when the government needs to enter into contracts quickly in response to natural disasters or combat operations. The third exception addresses situations akin to dual sourcing, when the government attempts to manage the industrial base by ensuring that companies receive enough orders to stay in business. The fifth exception includes purchases that agencies are required to make through Federal Prison Industries or qualified nonprofit agencies for the blind or "severely disabled."[62]

Despite covering many common situations, CICA's exceptions do not grant agencies unfettered discretion to contract for goods and services without using competitive procedures, however. This is because other provisions of CICA impose several conditions on agencies' ability to rely on the exceptions permitting other than full and open competition. What is arguably the most important of these conditions—the requirement that agency contracting officials justify and obtain approval for their use of other than competitive procedures—is discussed in more detail in the following section. Other conditions (1) specify that poor agency planning cannot give rise to unusual and compelling urgency;[63] (2) bar agencies from obtaining through other agencies goods or services that were not obtained in compliance with CICA;[64] (3) prohibit agency heads from delegating their authority to determine that use of other than competitive procedures is necessary in the public interest;[65] and (4) require agencies to "request offers from as many potential sources as is practicable under the circumstances" whenever relying on the exceptions for unusual and compelling urgency or national security.[66] The first condition is especially important because it precludes agencies from waiting until near the end of the fiscal year to procure items and then claiming unusual and compelling urgency because their appropriations are about to expire.[67]

Justifications & Approvals

CICA's requirement that contracting officers provide justifications of, and obtain approvals for, all noncompetitive procurements conducted in reliance on a CICA exception further checks agencies' discretion in using noncompetitive procedures.[68] Agencies can rely on the CICA exceptions only when contracting officers justify the use of other than competitive procedures in writing and certify the accuracy and completeness of their justifications.[69] These justifications must then be approved by agency officials of a higher rank than the contracting officer, with the identity of the approving official determined by the expected value of the contract,[70] as *Table 1* illustrates.

Table 1.Approving Officials for Noncompetitive Contracts in General

Contract Value	Approving Official
Under $650,000	Contracting officer's certification suffices unless higher approval is required under agency procedures
Over $650,000 and below $12.5 million	Competition advocate for the procuring activity or another official as provided under 48 C.F.R. §6.304(a)(3) or (4) (authority cannot be delegated)
Over $12.5 million and below $62.5 million (all agencies other than DOD, NASA, and the Coast Guard) Over $12.5 million and below $85.5 million (DOD, NASA, and the Coast Guard)	Head of the procuring activity or a delegate who, if a member of the armed services, is a general or flag officer or, if a civilian, is serving in a GS-16 or higher position or a comparable position under another schedule
Over $62.5 million (all agencies other than DOD, NASA, and the Coast Guard) Over $85.5 million (DOD, NASA, and the Coast Guard)	Senior procurement executive of the agency designated pursuant to Section 16(3) of the Office of Federal Procurement Policy Act (cannot be delegated, other than in the case of the Undersecretary of Defense for Acquisition, Technology & Logistics acting as the senior procurement executive of DOD)

Source: Congressional Research Service, based on 48 C.F.R. §6.304.

Written justifications and approvals must normally precede the contract award.[71] They may follow the award only when the agency relies on the exception for unusual and compelling urgency, and, even then, the agency must have determined the existence of usual and compelling urgency prior to making the award.[72] Justifications can be omitted only when an agency (1) relies upon an agency head's determination that it is necessary, in the public interest, to use other than competitive procedures; (2) conducts a procurement under the authority of the Javits-WagnerO'Day Act, or makes competitive or certain noncompetitive awards under the authority of Section 8(a) of the Small Business Act;[73] or (3) purchases brand-name items for authorized resale.[74] The omission of justifications when the agency relies upon the agency head's determination that it is necessary, in the public interest, to use other than competitive procedures can be explained, in part, by the requirement that agency heads must themselves document the existence of such circumstances in writing and notify Congress. Purchase of brand-name items for authorized resale involves purchases for use in commissaries or similar facilities, where the purchased articles are "desired or preferred by customers of the selling activities."[75] It does not include agencies' purchase of brand-name commercial items for their own use.[76]

Justifications must include (1) a description of agency needs; (2) an identification of the statutory exception upon which the agency relied and a demonstration of the reasons for using the exception that is based upon the proposed contractor's qualifications or the nature of the procurement; (3) a determination that the anticipated cost will be fair and reasonable; (4) a description of any market survey conducted, or a statement of the reasons for not conducting a market survey; (5) a listing of any sources that expressed interest in the procurement in writing; and (6) a statement of any actions that the agency may take to remove or overcome barriers to competition before subsequent procurements.[77]

CICA originally required agencies to make their justifications for noncompetitive awards, as well as "any related information," available to the general public under the Freedom of Information Act (FOIA),[78] but it has since been amended to require that justifications and approvals be posted on FedBizOpps (http://www.fedbizopps.gov) within 14 days of contract award.[79] Agencies are also required, under CICA, to publish notices regarding certain noncompetitive contracts that they propose to award on FedBizOpps prior to their award.[80] These notices identify the intended recipient of the noncompetitive contract award and state the agencies' reasons for making a noncompetitive award.[81] Because notice of these proposed awards precedes the awards, other contractors could submit proposals to the agency or protest the proposed award.

"Special Simplified Procedures for Small Purchases"

In addition to authorizing the use of noncompetitive procedures in certain circumstances, CICA authorizes the use of "special simplified procedures" when agencies make "small purchases."[82] CICA's drafters included this provision because they recognized that the costs of conducting competitions can exceed the savings resulting from competition when agencies procure items with low prices.[83] CICA itself defined a "small purchase" as one whose expected value was less than $25,000,[84] but was later amended to include purchases whose expected value was below the simplified acquisition threshold (currently, generally $150,000).[85] Moreover, since 1996, under an amendment to CICA, agencies have also had authority to use simplified acquisition procedures in purchasing commercial items whose expected value exceeds the simplified acquisition threshold but is below $6.5 million (or $12 million in the case of goods or services purchased in support of contingency operations, or for defense against or recovery from nuclear, biological, chemical, or radiological attack).[86] Agencies can rely on this latter authority only when their contracting officers reasonably expect, based upon market research and the nature of the goods or services sought, that offers will include only commercial items.[87] This authority to use simplified procedures in purchases of commercial items valued at between $150,000 and $6.5 million is temporary, under what the Federal Acquisition Regulation (FAR) calls a "test program," and expires on January 1, 2015, unless renewed.[88] CICA prohibits agencies from dividing proposed purchases in excess of the "small purchase" threshold into several purchases in order to take advantage of the simplified procedures, and it requires agencies to promote competition "to the maximum extent practicable" when using simplified procedures.[89]

CICA otherwise leaves the articulation of the simplified acquisition procedures to the FAR, which prescribes somewhat different regulations for acquiring different prices and types of goods and services (i.e., commercial or noncommercial). See *Figure 1*. Under the FAR, purchases whose expected value is below the simplified acquisition threshold ($150,000) are further subdivided into (1) those below the micropurchase threshold (generally $3,000) and (2) those above it.[90] When making "micropurchases," or purchases at or below $3,000, agencies are to promote competition, to at least a limited degree, by distributing their purchases "equitably" among qualified suppliers "[t]o the extent practicable."[91] They may make micropurchases without soliciting competitive quotations only if the contracting officer, or other duly appointed official, considers the price to be reasonable.[92] When purchases are above the micropurchase threshold but below the simplified acquisition threshold, agencies "shall use simplified acquisition procedures to the maximum extent practicable."[93] These purchases are "reserved exclusively" for small businesses,[94] making them "competitive procedures" under CICA. In such purchases, and in purchases of commercial items whose expected value exceeds the simplified acquisition threshold but is below $6.5 million (or $12 million in emergencies), agencies "must promote competition to the maximum extent practicable to obtain supplies and services from the source whose offer is the most advantageous to the Government, considering the administrative cost of the purchase."[95] This generally means that agencies "must consider solicitation of at least three sources," two of which were not included in the previous solicitation.[96] Contracting officers are prohibited from soliciting quotations based on personal preferences or restricting solicitations to suppliers of well-known and widely distributed makes or brands.[97]

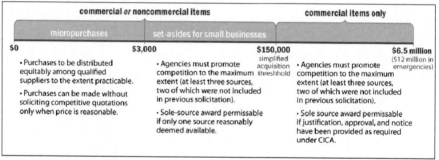

Source: Congressional Research Service.

Figure 1. Simplified Acquisition Procedures: Competition Requirements at Various Price Thresholds.

Table 2. Approving Officials for Noncompetitive Contracts Under the Simplified Acquisition Procedures

Contract Value	Approving Official
Over $150,000 and below $650,000	Contracting officer's certification serves as approval unless agency regulations require higher-level approval
Over $650,000 and below $12.5 million	Competition advocate for the procuring activity, or an official described in 48 C.F.R. §6.304(a)(3)-(4) (cannot be delegated)
Over $12.5 million and below $62.5 million (all agencies other than DOD, NASA, and the Coast Guard) Over $12.5 million and below $85.5 million (DOD, NASA, and the Coast Guard)	Head of the procuring activity, or an official described in 48 C.F.R. §6.304(a)(3)-(4) (cannot be delegated)
Over $62.5 million (all agencies other than DOD, NASA, and the Coast Guard)	Official described in 48 C.F.R. §6.304(a)(4) (cannot be delegated other than as provided in 48 C.F.R. §6.304(a)(4))
Over $85.5 million (DOD, NASA, and the Coast Guard)	

Source: Congressional Research Service, based on 48 C.F.R. §13.501(a)(2).

Sole-source solicitations for purchases below the simplified acquisition threshold are permissible only if contracting officers determine that the circumstances of the contract action are such that only one source can be reasonably deemed available (e.g., urgency, exclusive licensing agreements, brand-name goods, industrial mobilization).[98] Sole-source solicitations for purchases of commercial items whose expected costs exceed the simplified acquisition threshold are permissible only if (1) they are justified in writing; (2) they are approved at the levels specified in *Table 2*; and (3) notice of the proposed award is provided at the government-wide point of entry, FedBizOpps.[99]

Table 3. Types of Competition Under CICA

Competition Type	Includes
Full and Open Competition	Sealed bids Competitive proposals Other competitive procedures (e.g., GSA's Federal Supply Schedule) Full and open competition after the exclusion of sources Dual sourcing Set-asides for small businesses[a]
Permissibly Noncompetitive	Sole source (including sole-source awards to small businesses)a Unusual and compelling urgency Maintenance of the industrial base International agreements Statutory requirements or brand-name items for resale National security Necessary in the public interest
Special Simplified Procedures	Micropurchases (noncommercial or commercial items) Purchases above the micropurchase threshold but below the simplified acquisition threshold ($150,000) (noncommercial or commercial items) → reserved for small businesses Purchases of commercial items whose prices are between $150,000 and $6.5 million (or $12 million in emergencies)

Source: Congressional Research Service.

[a] CICA generally classifies contracts with small businesses in two different ways, depending upon whether the contract is a sole-source award. Under CICA, sole-source awards to small businesses are generally permissible in light of the circumstances permitting other than full and open competition, while other awards to small businesses result from "full and open competition after exclusion of sources." However, sole-source awards to small businesses owned by Alaska

Native Corporations or Indian Tribes participating in the Small Business Administration's Minority Small Business and Capital Ownership Development Program (commonly known as the "8(a) Program") are a bit different in that they are noncompetitive procedures expressly authorized by statute.

Other Competition Requirements

In keeping with its drafters' belief that effective competition in government procurement involves more than just the mechanisms that agencies use to solicit offers, CICA also contains other provisions that promote competition by, among other things, barring agencies from using restrictive specifications and requiring them to give advance notice of upcoming solicitations.[100] These provisions are not the primary focus of this report, but are briefly summarized below in order to provide a complete sense of CICA's competition requirements.

1) *Planning and solicitation requirements*: Under CICA, agencies must specify their needs and solicit bids or offers "in a manner designed to achieve full and open competition"; use advanced procurement planning and market research; and "develop specifications in such a manner as is necessary to obtain full and open competition."[101] Specifications may be stated in terms of function, performance, or design requirements, but can include restrictive provisions or conditions only to the extent necessary to satisfy agency needs or as authorized by law.[102] These requirements derive from the fact that competitive mechanisms for submitting bids or offers are of limited effectiveness if agencies can craft their procurement specifications in such a way as to effectively exclude contractors from the pool of potential offerors.[103]

2) *Evaluation and award requirements*: Agencies must evaluate sealed bids and competitive proposals based solely on the factors specified in the solicitation.[104] This requirement supports the competitive mechanisms for submitting bids and offers by ensuring that agencies properly consider bids and offers once they are received, rather than award contracts to favored companies on the basis of factors not disclosed to other competitors.

3) *Competition advocates*: CICA requires the head of each executive agency to designate, both for the agency as a whole and for each

procuring activity within the agency, one officer or employee to serve as the "advocate for competition."[105] Agency competition advocates are responsible, among other things, for challenging barriers to and promoting full and open competition in agency procurement activities.[106] CICA initially required agency competition advocates to make annual reports to each chamber of Congress identifying actions the agency intended to take to increase competition for contracts and reduce the number and value of noncompetitive contracts.[107] However, FASA removed this reporting requirement.[108]

4) Procurement notices: Under CICA, agencies are generally required to publish "procurement notices" announcing upcoming IFBs and RFPs for contracts exceeding $25,000 and for likely subcontracts on awarded contracts exceeding $25,000.[109] CICA also specifies that agencies may not issue solicitations earlier than 15 days after the notice is published, or establish a deadline for submission of bids or offers earlier than 30 days after the solicitation is issued.[110] These requirements promote competition by ensuring that would-be offerors have ample notice of proposed agency procurement actions and adequate time to prepare their offers. Notices were originally published in Commerce Business Daily, but are now posted online at FedBizOpps.[111]

COMPETITION REQUIREMENTS FOR TASK AND DELIVERY ORDER CONTRACTS

FASA supplemented CICA by, among other things, articulating competition requirements for task order and delivery order (TO/DO) contracts. TO/DO contracts are contracts for services or goods, respectively, that do not "procure or specify a firm quantity of supplies (other than a minimum or maximum quantity)," but rather "provide[] for the issuance of orders for the delivery of supplies during the period of the contract."[112] Because the time of delivery and the quantity of goods or services to be delivered are not specified (outside of stated maximums or minimums) in TO/DO contracts, such contracts are sometimes referred to as indefinite delivery/indefinite quantity (ID/IQ) contracts.[113] TO/DO contracts are also known as single-award or multiple-award contracts, a designation based upon the number of firms—one or more than one, respectively— able to compete for task or delivery orders under the contract.[114] Some commentators further refer to single-award TO/DO contracts as "monopoly contracts,"[115] but such usage could obscure the fact that single-award TO/DO contracts are themselves awarded competitively, even if task or delivery orders under them are not, and are of limited duration.[116]

Under FASA, agencies are effectively subject to CICA when awarding TO/DO contracts and can use other than competitive procedures only when one of the seven exceptions to full and open competition applies and there are the requisite justifications and approvals.[117] FASA also establishes "a preference" for multiple-award contracts by requiring agencies to use them, as opposed to single-award contracts, "to the maximum extent practicable."[118] Moreover, FASA requires agencies using multiple-award contracts to provide contractors "a fair opportunity to be considered" when issuing task or delivery orders in excess of $3,000 unless

1) the agency's need for the services or property is of such unusual urgency that providing such opportunity to all such contractors would result in unacceptable delays in fulfilling that need;
2) only one such contractor is capable of providing the services or property required at the level of quality required because the services or property ordered are unique or highly specialized;
3) the task or delivery order should be issued on a sole-source basis in the interest of economy and efficiency because it is a logical follow-on to a task or delivery order already issued on a competitive basis; or
4) it is necessary to place the order with a particular contractor in order to satisfy a minimum guarantee.[119]

FASA did not, however, subject the issuance of task or delivery orders under TO/DO contracts to CICA, and, even today, such orders remain outside the CICA framework.[120] FASA further requires each agency issuing TO/DO contracts to designate a "task and delivery order ombudsman" to review contractors' complaints regarding TO/DO contracts and ensure that all contractors holding a multiple-award TO/DO contract have a "fair opportunity to be considered" for orders.[121] Finally, FASA grants the Government Accountability Office (GAO) jurisdiction over protests alleging that the orders increase the scope, period, or maximum value of the contract.[122]

The National Defense Authorization Act for FY2008 (NDAA '08) further strengthened the competition requirements for TO/DO contracts established by

FASA. See *Figure 2*. The NDAA '08 limits agencies' ability to use single-award TO/DO contracts by requiring that agency heads make the following determinations, in writing, before awarding a single-award TO/DO contract whose expected value would exceed $103 million, including options:

i.   the task or delivery orders expected under the contract are so integrally related that only a single source can reasonably perform the work;

ii. the contract provides only for firm, fixed-price task or delivery orders for (I) products for which unit prices are established in the contract or (II) services for which prices are established in the contract for the specific tasks to be performed;

iii. only one source is qualified and capable of performing the work at a reasonable price to the government; or

iv. because of exceptional circumstances, it is necessary in the public interest to award the contract to a single source.[123]

The NDAA '08 also specifies what constitutes a "fair opportunity to be considered" in competitions for orders in excess of $5.5 million under multiple-award TO/DO contracts. Under the NDAA, for contractors to have a fair opportunity, agencies must provide them with (1) a notice of the task or delivery order that includes a clear statement of the agency's requirements; (2) a reasonable period of time to provide a proposal in response to the notice; (3) disclosure of the significant factors and subfactors (including cost or price) that the agency expects to consider in evaluating proposals and their relative importance; (4) a written statement documenting the basis for the award and the relative importance of quality and price or cost factors, if the award is to be made on a best-value basis; and (5) an opportunity for post-award debriefing.[124]

Finally, the NDAA '08 granted GAO exclusive authority to hear protests alleging improprieties in agencies' award of task and delivery orders valued in excess of $10 million that do not increase the scope, period, or maximum value of the underlying contract.[125] When granting such authority, Congress initially included a "sunset" provision, stating that the "subsection" granting this authority would be "in effect for three years, beginning on the date that it is 120 days after [its] date of enactment" (i.e., May 27, 2011).[126] However, the 112th Congress subsequently granted GAO permanent jurisdiction over the protests of "large" orders issued under defense contracts.[127] It also extended

GAO's jurisdiction over similar orders issued under civilian contracts through September 30, 2016.[128]

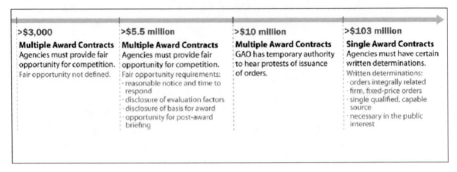

>$3,000	>$5.5 million	>$10 million	>$103 million
Multiple Award Contracts	**Multiple Award Contracts**	**Multiple Award Contracts**	**Single Award Contracts**
Agencies must provide fair opportunity for competition.	Agencies must provide fair opportunity for competition.	GAO has temporary authority to hear protests of issuance of orders.	Agencies must have certain written determinations.
Fair opportunity not defined.	Fair opportunity requirements: · reasonable notice and time to respond · disclosure of evaluation factors · disclosure of basis for award · opportunity for post-award briefing		Written determinations: · orders integrally related · firm, fixed-price orders · single qualified, capable source · necessary in the public interest

Source: Congressional Research Service.

Figure 2. TO/DO Contracts: Competition Requirements at Various Price Thresholds.

End Notes

[1] Ralph C. Nash, Jr., Steve L. Schooner, Karen R. O'Brien-DeBakey, and Vernon J. Edwards, THE GOVERNMENT CONTRACTS REFERENCE BOOK: A COMPREHENSIVE GUIDE TO THE LANGUAGE OF PROCUREMENT 109-110 (2d ed. 2007).

[2] See, e.g., Gates Cites Acquisition Reform as One of Defense Department's Greatest Challenges, 91 FED. CONT. R. 71 (February 3, 2009) (then-Secretary of Defense Robert Gates emphasizing increased competition as a potential source of savings for the Department).

[3] The White House, Office of the Press Secretary, Government Contracting: Memorandum for the Heads of Executive Departments and Agencies, March 4, 2009, available at http://www.whitehouse.gov/the_press_office/Memorandumfor-the-Heads-of-Executive-Departments-and-Agencies-Subject-Government/.

[4] Executive Office of the President, Office of Management and Budget, Increasing Competition and Structuring Contracts for Best Results, October 27, 2009 (copy on file with the author) (also calling for agencies to focus on requirements development and outreach to potential vendors, use performance-based acquisitions and commercial solutions, and engage in strategic sourcing, among other things).

[5] Prime Award Spending Data, Federal Spending FY2011: Contracts, available at http://usaspending.gov/explore? carryfilters=on.

[6] See 48 C.F.R. §214.201-6 (sealed bidding); 48 C.F.R. §§215.317-1—215.317-5 (negotiated procurement). See also Office of the Undersecretary of Defense for Acquisition, Technology and Logistics, Review Criteria for the Acquisition of Services: Memorandum, February 18, 2009, available at http://www.acq.osd.mil/dpap/policy/policyvault/USA002735-08-DPAP.pdf (stating that the requirements of service contracts should be articulated in such a way as to provide for "maximum competition," in general, and for "meaningful competition" for orders under multiple award contracts).

[7] See, e.g., National Defense Authorization Act for FY2012, P.L. 112-81, §141, 125 Stat. 1324 (December 31, 2011) ("Of the funds authorized to be appropriated by this Act or otherwise

made available for fiscal year 2012 for other procurement, for covered programs of the joint tactical radio system, not more than 70 percent may be obligated or expended until the date on which the Secretary of the Army submits to the congressional defense committees written certification that the acquisition strategy for the full-rate production of covered programs of such radio system includes full and open competition ... that includes commercially developed systems that the Secretary determines are qualified with respect to successful testing by the Army and certification by the National Security Agency."); id., §215, 125 Stat. 1333 (similar requirements as to research and development for the F-35 Lightning II aircraft program); id., §353, 125 Stat. 1376-77 (similar requirements as to the Army's migration to enterprise email systems).

[8] See, e.g., id., §844, 125 Stat. 1515 (requiring the Secretary of Defense to establish goals for competition in contracts for goods or services to be used outside the United States in support of a contingency operation).

[9] See, e.g., id.

[10] See, e.g., id. (requiring a DOD competition advocate to report annually on the Logistics Civil Augmentation Program (LOGCAP) contract or any "similar omnibus contract" awarded by the Department for goods or services to be used outside the United States in support of a contingency operation); Consolidated Appropriations Act, 2012, P.L. 112-74, §520, 125 Stat. 972-73 (December 23, 2011) (requiring the Inspector General of the Department of Homeland Security to review selected contracts awarded in the previous year through means other than full and open competition and report to Congress).

[11] P.L. 112-74, §8036, 125 Stat. 813. See also P.L. 112-81, §222, 125 Stat. 1336 (authorizing the Secretary of the Army to conduct a program for flight research and demonstration of advanced rotorcraft technology, but requiring that the Secretary comply with the Competition in Contracting Act (CICA) when awarding a contract under this authority).

[12] See, e.g., P.L. 112-81, §837, 125 Stat. 1509 (amending the Weapon Systems Acquisition Reform Act (WSARA) of 2009 to incorporate operation, as well as sustainment of major weapon systems, subsystems of major weapons systems, and components needed for maintenance and sustainment of such systems). WSARA called for the Secretary of Defense to "ensure that the acquisition strategy for each major defense acquisition program includes ... measures to ensure competition, or the option of competition, ... throughout the life-cycle of [the] program as a means to improve contractor performance." See P.L. 111-23, §202(a)(1), 123 Stat. 1720-21 (May 22, 2009).

[13] See, e.g., P.L. 112-74, §7082, 125 Stat. 1261-62 (prohibiting the disbursement of funds appropriated under this act for a U.S. contribution to the general capital increases of the International Bank for Reconstruction and Development, the African Development Bank, or the Inter-American Development Bank until the Secretary of the Treasury reports to Congress that these entities are making "substantial progress" toward certain reforms, including "implementing procurement guidelines that maximize international competitive bidding in accordance with sound procurement practices, including transparency, competition, and cost-effective results for borrowers").

[14] See FAIR Act, P.L. 105-270, 112 Stat. 2382 (1998) (codified at 31 U.S.C. §501 note); Executive Office of the President, OMB, Performance of Commercial Activities: Circular A-76 Revised, May 29, 2003, available at http://www.whitehouse.gov/omb/circulars_a076_a76_incl_tech_correction.

[15] For more on public-private competitions generally, see CRS Report RL32079, Federal Contracting of Commercial Activities: Competitive Sourcing Targets, by L. Elaine Halchin.

[16] James F. Nagle, A HISTORY OF GOVERNMENT CONTRACTING 49 (2d ed. 1999).

[17] CICA was enacted as part of the Deficit Reduction Act of 1984, P.L. 98-369, §§2701-2753, 98 Stat. 1175 (1984). It amended the Armed Services Procurement Act of 1947; Federal Property and Administrative Services Act of 1949; Office of Federal Procurement Policy Act of 1974; and Truth in Negotiation Act (TINA) of 1962. It also created a statutory basis for the bid-protest function of the GAO. CICA's competition requirements took effect on April 1, 1985.

[18] COMPETITION IN CONTRACTING ACT OF 1983: HEARINGS BEFORE THE SENATE COMM. ON ARMED SERVICES, 98TH CONG., 1ST SESS. 260-61 (1983). The guidelines for implementing some of President Obama's recently proposed procurement reforms similarly call for "maximum practicable competition," rather than "maximum competition." See Executive Office of the President, Office of Management and Budget, Updated Implementing Guidance for the American Recovery and Reinvestment Act of 2009, at 52 (April 3, 2009), available at http://www.whitehouse.gov/ sites/default/files/ omb/assets/memoranda_fy2009/m09-15.pdf.

[19] COMPETITION IN CONTRACTING ACT OF 1983, supra note 18, at 304 (testimony of John Cibinic, Jr., Government Contracts Program, National Law Center, The George Washington University).

[20] William S. Cohen, The Competition in Contracting Act, 14 PUB. CONT. L.J. 1, 20-21 (1983/1984) ("Generally, agency officials have an easier time if they stay with the same contractor throughout the procurement process.").

[21] See id. at 6 (describing allegations of "war profiteering" in the aftermath of WWI); COMPETITION IN CONTRACTING ACT OF 1984: HEARINGS ON H.R. 5184 BEFORE THE SUBCOMM. ON LEGIS. & NAT'L SECURITY OF THE HOUSE COMM. ON GOV'T OPERATIONS, 98TH CONG., at 2 (1984) (statement by Representative Brooks) (describing how DOD spent $435 for "an ordinary claw hammer").

[22] The values contained in this chronology are those given in the statute as it was enacted. They do not reflect any subsequent adjustments made for inflation.

[23] 10 U.S.C. §2304(a)(1)(A) & 41 U.S.C. §3301(a)(1). Citations to CICA's codification generally reference two titles of the United States Code: Title 10 governing procurements by defense agencies, NASA, and the Coast Guard, and Title 41 governing procurements by civilian agencies. The numbering and language of these sections are often—but not always—identical.

[24] P.L. 103-355, §8104, 108 Stat. 3391 (codified at 10 U.S.C. §2377(a)-(b)); P.L. 103-355, §8203, 108 Stat. 3391 (codified at 41 U.S.C. §3307(c)(1) ("The head of each executive agency shall ensure that procurement officials in that executive agency, to the maximum extent practicable, acquire commercial items or nondevelopmental items other than commercial items to meet the needs of the executive agency.").

[25] P.L. 104-106, §4101, 110 Stat. 642 (February 10, 1996) (codified, in part, at 41 U.S.C. §3301(c)).

[26] P.L. 108-136, §§1401-1433, 117 Stat. 1664-1676 (November 23, 2003).

[27] P.L. 110-343, Title I, §107(a), 122 Stat. 3773 (October 3, 2008). The Secretary must transmit his or her determination, and its accompanying justification, to several congressional committees within 7 days.

[28] Some contracts entered into without full and open competition under the EESA have been of types traditionally "considered high risk for the government." Gov't Accountability Office, Troubled Asset Relief Program: Additional Actions Needed to Better Ensure Integrity, Accountability, and Transparency 38 (December 2008), available at http://www.gao.gov/ products/GAO-09-161.

[29] In introducing the circumstances permitting use of noncompetitive procedures, CICA does not speak of "exceptions" to its competition requirements. See 10 U.S.C. §2304(c) & 41 U.S.C. §3304(a). However, it uses the term "exception" in reference to these circumstances in its requirement for justifications and approvals of contracts awarded using other than full and open competition, and commentators commonly refer to the "CICA exceptions" when describing these circumstances. See 10 U.S.C. §2304(f)(3)(B) & 41 U.S.C. §3304(e)(2)(B).

[30] 10 U.S.C. §2304(a)(1)(A) & 41 U.S.C. §3301(a).

[31] GOVERNMENT CONTRACTS REFERENCE BOOK, supra note 1, at 414.

[32] For more on OTA generally, see CRS Report RL34760, Other Transaction (OT) Authority, by L. Elaine Halchin.

[33] 10 U.S.C. §2304(a)(1)(A); 41 U.S.C. §3301(a). CICA also does not apply to contract modifications, including the exercise of price options evaluated as part of the initial competition, that are within the scope of existing contracts, or orders under requirements contracts or definite-quantity contracts. 48 C.F.R. §6.001(a)-(f).

[34] P.L. 108-447, Division D, §534(e), 118 Stat. 2809, 3006 (December 8, 2004).

[35] Id. at Division E, Title I, 118 Stat. 3040 (allowing the Bureau of Land Management to limit competition for contracts for hazardous fuel reduction activities to specified groups or entities, notwithstanding CICA); id. at Division E, Title II, 118 Stat. 3089 (allowing the National Gallery of Art to contract for the restoration and repair without competition).

[36] 10 U.S.C. §2304(a)(1)(A) & 41 U.S.C. §3301(a)(1).

[37] 10 U.S.C. §2304(a)(1)(A) & 41 U.S.C. §3301(a)(1) (requirement for full and open competition); 10 U.S.C. §2304(c) & 41 U.S.C. §3304(a) (circumstances allowing use of other than competitive procedures).

[38] 41 U.S.C. §107.

[39] 41 U.S.C. §113(1)-(7). For more information on the "responsibility" requirements applicable to prospective federal contractors, see CRS Report R40633, Responsibility Determinations Under the Federal Acquisition Regulation: Legal Standards and Procedures, by Kate M. Manuel.

[40] CICA defines "competitive procedures" as those under which an agency enters into a contract pursuant to full and open competition. 41 U.S.C. §§152, 3301.

[41] 48 C.F.R. §14.101(a)-(e).

[42] 10 U.S.C. §2304(a)(2)(A)(i)-(iv) & 41 U.S.C. §3301(b)(1)(A)(i)-(iv).

[43] 10 U.S.C. §2304(a)(2)(B) & 41 U.S.C. §3301(b)(1)(B).

[44] 48 C.F.R. §§15.000-15.102. "Best value" is determined by considering price and other factors included in the solicitation. The "competitive range" consists of those proposals having the greatest likelihood of award based on the factors and significant sub-factors of the solicitation. FARA allows agencies to limit the competitive range to those offerors rated most highly based upon the solicitation's criteria when "the number of offers that would otherwise be included in the competitive range ... exceeds the number at which an efficient competition can be conducted." P.L. 104- 106, §4103, 110 Stat. 643-44 (February 10, 1996) (codified at 10 U.S.C. §2305(b) & 41 U.S.C. §3703(b)).

[45] 41 U.S.C. §152(4).

[46] 48 C.F.R. §8.402(a).

[47] For more on small business set-asides, see generally CRS Report R41945, Small Business Set-Aside Programs: An Overview and Recent Developments in the Law, by Kate M. Manuel and Erika K. Lunder.

[48] 10 U.S.C. §2304(b) & 41 U.S.C. §3303.

[49] 10 U.S.C. §2304(b)(1)-(2) & 41 U.S.C. §3303(a)-(b). In practice, there is one important distinction between "full and open competition after exclusion of sources" for purposes of dual sourcing and for small business set-asides. Agencies engaged in dual sourcing need justifications and approvals for their awards, which are discussed in more detail below, while those setting aside procurements for small businesses generally do not. Compare 48 C.F.R. §6.202(b)(1) (dual sourcing) with 48 C.F.R. §6.203(b), §6.204(b), §6.205(b), §6.206(b), and §6.207(b) (small business set-asides). Only when agencies make sole-source awards in excess of $20 million under the authority of Section 8(a) of the Small Business Act are justifications and approvals required. See P.L. 111-84, §811, 123 Stat. 2405-06 (October 28, 2009).

[50] See, e.g., Competition in Contracting Act, supra note 20, at 25-26.

[51] 10 U.S.C. §2304(b)(1)(A)-(F) & 41 U.S.C. §3303(a)(1)(A)-(F). CICA added the provisions currently in subsections (A)-(C) of these statutes, while FARA added those in (D)-(F).

[52] See, e.g., P.L. 110-181, §213, 122 Stat. 36 (October 14, 2008) (requiring DOD to "ensure the obligation and expenditure in each such fiscal year of sufficient annual amounts for the continued development and procurement of 2 options for the propulsion system for the Joint Strike Fighter in order to ensure the development and competitive production for the propulsion system for the Joint Strike Fighter."); Gates Says Tanker Competition May Resume in Late Spring; Murtha Endorses "Split Buy," 91 FED. CONTR. R. 75 (February 3, 2009).

[53] 10 U.S.C. §2304(b)(2) & 41 U.S.C. §3303(b).

[54] See 15 U.S.C. §637(a) (set-asides for small disadvantaged businesses participating in the 8(a) Business Development Program); 15 U.S.C. §637(m) (set-asides for women-owned small businesses); 15 U.S.C. §644 (set-asides for small businesses generally); 15 U.S.C. §657a (set-asides for HUBZone small businesses); 15 U.S.C. §657f (set-asides for service-disabled veteran-owned small businesses).

[55] The Stafford Act provides that "[i]n the expenditure of Federal funds for debris clearance, distribution of supplies, reconstruction, and other major disaster or emergency assistance activities ... carried out by contract or agreement with private [entities], preference shall be given, to the extent feasible and practicable, to those organizations, firms, and individuals residing or doing business primarily in the area affected by such major disaster or emergency." 42 U.S.C. §5150(a)(1).

[56] 10 U.S.C. §2304(c) & 41 U.S.C. §§152, 3301(a).

[57] 10 U.S.C. §2304(c) & 41 U.S.C. §3304(c).

[58] An amendment made to CICA by Section 862 of the Duncan Hunter National Defense Authorization Act for FY2009 limits the duration of contracts awarded in reliance on this exception. The term of such contracts may not exceed the time necessary (1) to meet the unusual and compelling requirements of the work to be performed under the contract and (2) for the executive agency to enter into another contract for the required goods and services through the use of competitive procedures. Such contracts may not last longer than one year unless the head of the agency entering into the contract determines that exceptional circumstances apply. P.L. 110-417, §862, 122 Stat. 4546 (October 14, 2008).

[59] 10 U.S.C. §2304(c)(1)-(7) & 41 U.S.C. §3304(1)(1)-(7).

[60] See, e.g., U.S. House of Representatives, Comm. on Gov't Reform—Minority Staff, Special Investigations Division, Dollars, Not Sense: Government Contracting Under the Bush Administration 9 (2006), available at http://oversightarchive.waxman.house.gov/documents/20061211100757-98364.pdf.

[61] 10 U.S.C. §2304(d)(1)(A)-(B) & 41 U.S.C. §3304(b)(1)-(2). A follow-on contract is a new contract awarded on a sole-source basis to a contractor that previously had a design or manufacturing contract for the same item, or previously performed the services being procured. It differs from an option under an existing contract, which gives the government a unilateral right to purchase additional supplies or services under a contract, or otherwise extend a contract.

[62] See generally 48 C.F.R. §§8.601-8.716.

[63] 10 U.S.C. §2304(f)(5)(A) & 41 U.S.C. §3304(f)(5)(A)(i). See, e.g., RBC Bearings Inc., Comp. Gen. Dec. B-401661 (October 27, 2009) (sustaining a protest of sole-source contract award because the procuring agency's own poor planning resulted in the need to limit competition).

[64] 10 U.S.C. §2304(f)(5)(B) & 41 U.S.C. §3304(f)(5)(A)(ii).

[65] 10 U.S.C. §2304(d)(2) & 41 U.S.C. §3304(a)(7).

[66] 10 U.S.C. §2304(e) & 41 U.S.C. §3304(d). Under the FAR, similar requirements apply to all the CICA exceptions. See 48 C.F.R. §6.301(d).

[67] See, e.g., Competition in Contracting Act, supra note 20, at 16-17 (describing how agencies reportedly abused their authority, under the pre-CICA competition requirements, to make noncompetitive procurements when "competition is impracticable" in similar situations).

[68] 10 U.S.C. §2304(f) & 41 U.S.C. §3304(e).

[69] 10 U.S.C. §2304(f)(1)(A) & 41 U.S.C. §3304(e)(1)(A).

[70] 10 U.S.C. §2304(f)(1)(B) & 41 U.S.C. §3304(e)(1)(B)(i)-(iii).

[71] 10 U.S.C. §2304(f)(2) & 41 U.S.C. §3304(e)(3).

[72] 48 C.F.R. §6.303-1(e).

[73] Justifications, approvals, and notices are, however, required when agencies make sole-source awards valued in excess of $20 million under the authority of Section 8(a) of the Small Business Act. See P.L. 111-84, §811, 123 Stat. 2405-06 (October 28, 2009).

[74] 10 U.S.C. §2304(f)(2)(A)-(E) & 41 U.S.C. §3304(e)(4)(A)-(D).

[75] 48 C.F.R. §6.302-5(c)(3).

[76] Such purchases are governed by other authorities. See 48 C.F.R. §11.105.

[77] 10 U.S.C. §2304(f)(3)(A)-(F) & 41 U.S.C. §3304(e)(2)(A)-(F).

[78] P.L. 98-369, §2711, 98 Stat. 1178 (civilian agencies); id., at §2723, 98 Stat. 1190 (defense agencies).

[79] P.L. 110-181, §844, 122 Stat. 236-39 (October 14, 2008). When the noncompetitive award is made on the basis of unusual and compelling urgency, agencies have up to 30 days after the award to post it on FedBizOpps.

[80] 10 U.S.C. §2304(f)(1)(C) & 41 U.S.C. §3304(e)(1)(C). See generally 41 U.S.C. §1708(b)(2) (notice requirements).

[81] Id.

[82] 10 U.S.C. §2304(g)(1)(A) & 41 U.S.C. §3305.

[83] See, e.g., COMPETITION IN CONTRACTING ACT OF 1984, supra note 21, at 226. For example, spending $50 to achieve full and open competition saves money when the competition reduces by 10% the price of goods or services costing $100,000, but not when it reduces by 10% the price of goods or services costing $10.

[84] P.L. 98-369 at §2711 and §2723.

[85] 10 U.S.C. §2304(g)(1)(A) & 41 U.S.C. §3305(a)(1). The simplified acquisition threshold is presently set at $150,000 unless there is an emergency. See 48 C.F.R. §2.101 (increasing the threshold to $300,000, for contracts to be awarded or performed within the United States,

and $1 million for contracts to be awarded or performed outside the United States, in certain emergencies).

[86] 48 C.F.R. §13.500(a) & (e).

[87] 10 U.S.C. §2304(g)(1)(B) & 41 U.S.C. §3305(a)(2).

[88] 48 C.F.R. §13.500(d). FARA created this authority, which has been repeatedly renewed. See P.L. 104-106, at §4202 (establishing the authority); National Defense Authorization Act for FY2000, P.L. 106-65, §806 (extension through January 1, 2002); National Defense Authorization Act for FY2002, P.L. 107-107, §823 (extension through January 1, 2003); Bob Stump National Defense Authorization Act for FY2003, P.L. 107-314, §812 (extension through January 1, 2004); National Defense Authorization Act for FY2004, P.L. 108-136, §1442 (extension through January 1, 2006); and Ronald W. Reagan National Defense Authorization Act for FY2005, P.L. 108-375, §817 (extension through January 1, 2008); National Defense Authorization Act for FY2008, P.L. 110-181, §822 (extension through January 1, 2010); National Defense Authorization Act for FY2010, P.L. 111-84, §816 (extension through January 1, 2012); National Defense Authorization Act for FY2013, P.L. 112-239, §822, __ Stat. __ (January 2, 2013). The Bush Administration's reliance on this authority proved controversial, but the Obama Administration has also relied on it. See Dollars, Not Sense, supra note 60, at 18; Executive Office of the President, Office of Management and Budget, Initial Implementing Guidance for the American Recovery and Reinvestment Act of 2009, at 42 (February 18, 2009), available at http://www.recovery.gov/ files/Initial%20Recovery%20Act%20Implementing%20Guidance.pdf.

[89] 10 U.S.C. §2304(g)(3) & 41 U.S.C. §3305(c).

[90] The micropurchase threshold can be lower or higher than $3,000, depending on the goods or services acquired and the circumstances of the acquisition. Micropurchases for construction services subject to the Davis-Bacon Act or other services subject to the Service Contract Act have lower limits: $2,000 and $2,500, respectively. Those for goods or services that the agency head has determined will be used to support a contingency operation or facilitate defense against or recovery from nuclear, biological, chemical, or radiological attack have higher limits: $15,000 in the case of contracts to be awarded or performed, or purchases to be made, inside the United States and $30,000 in the case of contracts to be awarded or performed, or purchases to be made, outside the United States. 48 C.F.R. §13.201(g)(1)(i)-(ii).

[91] 48 C.F.R. §13.202(a)(1).

[92] 48 C.F.R. §13.202(a)(2).

[93] 48 C.F.R. §13.003(a). This provision does not apply if agencies can meet their requirements using (1) required sources of supply under Part 8 of the FAR (addressing Federal Prison Industries; the Committee for Purchase from People Who Are Blind or Severely Disabled, and FSS contracts); (2) existing indefinite delivery/indefinite quantity contracts; or (3) other existing contracts. 48 C.F.R. §13.003(a)(1)-(3).

[94] 48 C.F.R. §13.003(b)(1).

[95] 48 C.F.R. §13.104.

[96] 48 C.F.R. §13.104(b). When not providing notice of proposed contract actions and solicitation information through the government-wide point of entry, FedBizOpps, agencies can "ordinarily" obtain the "maximum practicable competition ... by soliciting quotations or offers from sources within the local trade area."

[97] 48 C.F.R. §13.104(a)(1)-(2).

[98] 48 C.F.R. §13.106-1(b)(1)(i).

[99] 48 C.F.R. §13.106-1(b)(2).

[100] See, e.g., Competition in Contracting Act, supra note 20, at 2 ("It is important to understand ... that competition is not a procurement procedure, but an objective which a procedure is designed to attain.").

[101] 10 U.S.C. §2305(a)(1)(A)(i)-(iii) & 41 U.S.C. §3306(a)(1)(A)-(C).

[102] 10 U.S.C. §2305(a)(1)(B)(i)-(ii) & 41 U.S.C. §3306(a)(2)(B) & (3)(A)-(C).

[103] See, e.g., Competition in Contracting Act, supra note 20, at 19 (describing specifications as the "cornerstone of competitive procurement" because they "serve initially as the fundamental expression of the agency's need and, in the contract award, as the baseline for the evaluation of offers.").

[104] 10 U.S.C. §2305(b); 41 U.S.C. §3306.

[105] 41 U.S.C. §1705(a)(2)(A).

[106] 41 U.S.C. §1705(b)(1)-(6).

[107] Agency competition requirements are, however, still required to complete an annual report for the agency's senior procurement executive. See 41 U.S.C. §1705(b)(4)(A)-(C).

[108] P.L. 103-355 §1031 (repealing subsection (c) of 10 U.S.C. §2318 and of 41 U.S.C. §419, which required annual reports on competition from defense and civilian agencies, respectively).

[109] 41 U.S.C. §1708.

[110] See 48 C.F.R. §5.203(a) & (d).

[111] See 48 C.F.R. §2.101 (defining "governmentwide point of entry" as the "single point where Government business opportunities greater than $25,000, including synopses of proposed contract actions, solicitations, and associated information, can be accessed electronically by the public. The GPE is located at http://www.fedbizopps.gov.").

[112] 48 C.F.R. §16.501-1.

[113] See 48 C.F.R. §16.501-2(a).

[114] Multiple-award task order contracts are sometimes also referred to as MATOCs.

[115] See, e.g., Dollars, Not Sense, supra note 60, at 13.

[116] Federal contracts are normally for one year, but can be extended to five years through agencies' use of options. 48 C.F.R. §17.204(e) ("Unless otherwise approved in accordance with agency procedures, the total of the basic and option periods shall not exceed 5 years in the case of services, and the total of the basic and option quantities shall not exceed the requirement for 5 years in the case of supplies.").

[117] 10 U.S.C. §2304a(c) & 41 U.S.C. §3304(a).

[118] 10 U.S.C. §2304a(d)(3) & 41 U.S.C. §4103(d)(4)(A).

[119] 10 U.S.C. §2304c(b)(1)-(4) & 41 U.S.C. §4106(c)(1)-(4).

[120] 48 C.F.R. §6.001(e)-(f).

[121] 10 U.S.C. §2304c(e) & 41 U.S.C. §4106(g).

[122] 10 U.S.C. §2304c(d) & 41 U.S.C. §4106(f).

[123] P.L. 110-181, §843, 122 Stat. 236-39 (October 14, 2008). Agency heads must notify Congress within 30 days after making a determination to award a single-award TO/DO contract in excess of $103 million. P.L. 110-181 addressed the TO/DO contracts of both defense and civilian agencies. An earlier law, the National Defense Authorization Act for Fiscal Year 2002, had addressed only DOD TO/DO contracts. This law required that the Defense Federal Acquisition Regulation Supplement (DFARS) be updated to (1) require that issuance of orders for services in excess of $100,000 under multiple award contracts be "competitive" unless a CICA exception applies and the agency issues a written justification and (2) specify what "competitive" means. See P.L. 107-107, §803, 115 Stat. 1179 (December 28, 2001).

[124] Id.

[125] Id.

[126] Id. at §843(a), 122 Stat. 237.

[127] National Defense Authorization Act for FY2013, P.L. 112-239, §830, __ Stat. __ (January 2, 2013).

[128] National Defense Authorization Act for FY2012, P.L. 112-81, §813, 125 Stat. 1491 (December 31, 2011) ("Paragraph (1)(B) and paragraph (2) of this subsection shall not be in effect after September 30, 2016."). For more on developments in the period between May 27, 2011, when the prior provision pertaining to the protests of orders issued under civilian agency contracts "sunset," and December 31, 2011, when this sunset date was extended until September 30, 2016, see CRS Report R42049, Jurisdiction over Challenges to "Large" Orders Under Federal Contracts, by Kate M. Manuel and Erika K. Lunder.

INDEX